CREATIVE
CONFLICT

CREATIVE

A PRACTICAL GUIDE FOR BUSINESS NEGOTIATORS

CONFLICT

BILL SANDERS | FRANK MOBUS

HARVARD BUSINESS REVIEW PRESS
BOSTON, MASSACHUSETTS

HBR Press Quantity Sales Discounts

Harvard Business Review Press titles are available at significant quantity discounts when purchased in bulk for client gifts, sales promotions, and premiums. Special editions, including books with corporate logos, customized covers, and letters from the company or CEO printed in the front matter, as well as excerpts of existing books, can also be created in large quantities for special needs.

For details and discount information for both print and ebook formats, contact booksales@harvardbusiness.org, tel. 800-988-0886, or www.hbr.org/bulksales.

The web addresses referenced in this book were live and correct at the time of the book's publication but may be subject to change.

Library of Congress Cataloging-in-Publication Data

Names: Sanders, Bill (William R.), author. | Mobus, Frank (Business consultant), author.
Title: Creative conflict : a practical guide for business negotiators / Bill Sanders, Frank Mobus.
Description: Boston, MA : Harvard Business Review Press, [2021] | Includes index.
Identifiers: LCCN 2020052658 (print) | LCCN 2020052659 (ebook) |
    ISBN 9781633699496 (hardcover) | ISBN 9781633699502 (ebook)
Subjects: LCSH: Negotiation in business. | Success in business. | Creative ability in business.
Classification: LCC HD58.6 .S27 2021 (print) | LCC HD58.6 (ebook) |
    DDC 658.4/052—dc23
LC record available at https://lccn.loc.gov/2020052658
LC ebook record available at https://lccn.loc.gov/2020052659

ISBN: 978-1-63369-949-6
eISBN: 978-1-63369-950-2

The paper used in this publication meets the requirements of the American National Standard for Permanence of Paper for Publications and Documents in Libraries and Archives Z39.48-1992.

For Barbara and Nina Mobus,
Frank's light and inspiration

CONTENTS

Part Four

The Partner
(RELATIONSHIP BUILDING)

Frank Mobus's Fundamental Insight

Some thirty years ago, a young Frank Mobus found himself on a panel with the venerable W. Edwards Deming, the management guru who inspired the post–World War II Japanese economic miracle. Deming transformed modern industry by solving a riddle: How does a company cut costs without compromising quality? The answer—the brainstorm that vaulted Toyota and Honda past GM and Ford—was to collaborate with the firm's Tier 1 suppliers, to work together to improve design, tooling, engineering, and so on down the line.

Deming frowned on mechanically awarding contracts to the lowest bidder. As he saw it, the art of procurement was to ferret out efficiencies and minimize *total* cost. His ideal was a quasi-partnership between buyers and trusted vendors, where everything was shared—even profits. Though Deming was best known for his systems for quality control and continuous improvement, his method could be distilled into one word: *teamwork*.

Toward the end of the panel session, Frank asked the great man: "How do two companies strike a balance between competition and cooperation?"

The Lion of Tokyo glared at Frank and roared, "Balance? Why the hell would you want balance? Just get rid of the competition!" A win-win fundamentalist, he believed that companies with strong relationships could transcend negotiating altogether.

Deming was on to something important, but he'd missed a crucial point. From the time we are born, our culture trains us to shy away from conflict. In business, arguments are typically seen as obstructive. It's human nature to covet applause, not debate. Out of fear of blowing up a meeting or a deal or a relationship, most of us soft-pedal discord as much as we can.

Yet consider:

John Lennon and Paul McCartney drove each other crazy. Their studio sessions were so tense and unpleasant that the audio engineer for *The White Album* quit midstream.

Bill Gates and Paul Allen were famous for their screaming matches, but their partnership hatched the software that launched the personal computer revolution.

James Watson and Frances Crick quarreled nonstop over the DNA molecule, but together they hit upon the double helix model that led to the Human Genome Project.

Magic Johnson and Larry Bird spurred one another to creative heights through their no-holds-barred, trash-talking rivalry on the basketball court.

Matisse and Picasso upset tradition from opposite directions. In their effort to one-up each other, they might paint the same subject—sometimes even with the same title. Matisse called their relationship a boxing match. As a critic wrote, "Picasso became Picasso because he would not let Matisse outshine him."[1]

In a study in *Basic and Applied Social Psychology,* seventy-four dating couples squared off in a simulated negotiation, with thirty-two mixed-sex pairs of complete strangers as a control group. Here's what the research found: The romantic couples "had lower outcome aspirations" and "less frequently generated offers which facilitate the discovery of mutually beneficial outcomes."[2] They were less aggressive and quicker to defer and agree—too quick, as it turned out, to grind their way to an out-of-the-box solution. The more fiercely committed the couple (as calibrated by "Rubin's love scale"), the *less* effectively they negotiated. The strangers were far superior collaborators. Their unchecked friction sparked better all-around deals.

Differences drive the creative process. From the time he earned his spurs, fresh out of college, by negotiating for his family construction firm, Frank Mobus understood something fundamental about business deals. There were any number of ways to manage competition between two parties, to modulate or perhaps subdue it, but you could never completely get rid of it. In Frank's view, conflict wasn't a hindrance to negotiating, nor even a necessary evil. He saw it as a goldmine of concealed value, an opportunity to find more profitable ways to satisfy both sides' needs.

Say you make a standing desk that you value at x, and I'm a wholesaler who values it at $2x$. Our subjective gap points us toward a mutually satisfying agreement. And if I can offer a service—like storage or transport—that costs me z, and you appraise it at $3z$, we'll be well on our way to enlarging our value pie.

But as Frank would remind us, the negotiation doesn't end there. We still must decide how the pie will be cut. We're obliged to keep the proceedings honest by competing for our fair shares. We need to collaborate *and* compete, at the same time.

Frank himself relished a hearty disagreement, be it about business or politics or the prospects of his beloved Los Angeles Clippers. He'd make his case with conviction and enthusiasm; he was an advocate at heart. But what made Frank unusual was that he'd truly *listen* to your response. He wasn't merely being polite. He was genuinely interested in what you had to say and whether you'd thought of something he had overlooked, because all of us have blind spots. He asked loads of questions; he had a gift for connecting with people and a curiosity about what made them tick. At the end of the day, he wouldn't necessarily agree with you, but he was always game for the discussion.

The germ of *Creative Conflict* was planted in the 1990s, when Frank took on an expanded role in content creation for Karrass, the late century's gold standard for business negotiation training. His progress accelerated in 2014, after we founded our own company. Faced with a blank canvas for a new seminar curriculum, Frank spent hours every day thinking, reading, writing, and debating with his close collaborators. Ideas poured out of him, and he had a knack for sparking our creativity as well. By the time his life was cut short in the summer of 2018 on a winding road in Maui, the content of this book was mostly in place.

Creative Conflict is the fruit of Frank's spirited exception to Deming and the *Getting to Yes* school, on the one hand, and the give-no-quarter combat of the early Karrass seminars on the other. It represents a third way of negotiating, an alternative to fight or flight, a richly textured middle ground. Like Adam Grant's "givers," creative negotiators enhance the process by focusing more on what people need from *them*. Neither partisans nor pushovers, they think before they act. They hear others out before they speak. Above all, they persist in wondering: *What if . . . ?*

In our hyperconnected, relentlessly disruptive business world, a two-sided arena of intense rivalry and deep cooperation, *Creative Conflict* is an idea whose time has urgently come.

—Bill Sanders

Part One

THE THIRD WAY

1

Negotiating a New Era

There was a time, not so long ago, when business negotiators followed a simple, linear roadmap. Their job wasn't always easy, but it was reasonably straightforward. Contracts were more or less uniform. Criteria were pretty much standard, with pricing first, second, and third. But that was then. In this more complex deal-making era, we're no longer comparing apples to apples. Modern buyers are eyeing Honeycrisps and Braeburns versus the latest Fuji–Golden Delicious hybrid, and asking themselves: *Exactly what kind of apple do we need?* And a seller might inquire: *Is it for eating or baking or juice? Do you want acidity or sweetness? How many days of shelf life? And what about bruising?* A thousand things need to be hashed out, and most of them aren't tied to dollar signs.

The art of negotiating is at a watershed. Over the last half-century, two polar philosophies have ruled the field: the win-lose combat taught by training wizard Chester Karrass, and the win-win creed of the mega-bestselling *Getting to Yes*. Both were leaps in their day. But neither fully meets the test of our volatile, disruptive, ultracompetitive world. In a time where problem-solving and problem-*finding* are of the essence, the old rules go out the window.

In short, it's time for something new. We wrote this book to show how negotiating is driven by competition *and* cooperation, often at the same time. It's a two-sided dance, and the choreography evolves as you move along. Creative business negotiating feeds on agility and invention. It flourishes with an openness to new ideas, no matter their source. Creative negotiators strive to expand a deal's scope while also pursuing a bigger portion of the pie. They push until they hit a wall of disagreement, and then they figure out how to get over it or through it or around it. They accept conflict as inevitable, and so it doesn't faze them. The less comfortable the dynamic, the greater the potential rewards.

When we tiptoe around our differences, we negotiate in a half-hearted way and get limited results. We won't find new opportunities by meekly deferring to the other side—or, on the other extreme, by steamrolling them into submission. Nor will we get there by sprinting to split the difference and be done with it. As the tale of Starbucks and United Airlines will illustrate in chapter 8, the best negotiators bring an appetite for contention, an eagerness to solve problems, and a willingness to persist and work the process as far as it can go.

Creative negotiators aren't easy marks—far from it. They exercise due diligence. If they run into deception or confrontational caveman tactics, they'll pull back to shield their organization's interests. But they also stand ready—when warranted—to shed their skepticism and meet the other party halfway, or maybe a little further. Step by calibrated step, taking smart and measured risks, they endeavor to build a more lasting, rewarding, comprehensive deal. Even at that point, however, they take nothing and no one for granted. They'll continue to monitor the other side's performance and weigh the deal's ever-shifting benefits against its costs. They know that negotiations continue long after a contract's ink has dried.

Creative Conflict is a practical user's guide that rests on two tentpole propositions. First, we'll show how the spectrum of business relationships demands a range of negotiating approaches. A one-and-done haggle relies upon a very different skill set than a long-term strategic alliance—the organizing principle of the Mobus Negotiating Continuum, to be addressed in our next chapter. Second, we'll explain why basic bargaining techniques, by themselves, won't guarantee success. Tactical proficiency is still necessary, but it's no longer sufficient; rules and tools are useless if we can't deploy them when it counts. Creative negotiators are attuned to their *mental model*, the lens through which they interpret events and relate to others. They guard against their weaknesses while capitalizing on their strengths. They control their emotions and keep their eyes on the prize: a bigger and better all-around deal for both sides.

With these two building blocks in place, you'll have the foundation you need to make the most out of any negotiation, whether it's a buy-sell transaction or an agreement to be navigated within your own organization.

Customized Competition

Through much of the twentieth century, the US economy was organized around standardized products for a generalized marketplace. Henry Ford liked to boast that you could buy a Model T in any color you wanted—as long as it was black. When Ford or General Motors needed paint or sparkplugs or tires, they issued a set of uniform specs for any suppliers who could meet them. Other industry leaders—DuPont, U.S. Steel, IBM—followed suit. Bidders were pitted one against the other, dragged down to their bottom line. In a page out of Thomas Hobbes, business-to-business negotiating was nasty, brutish, and short. The game was mechanical and impersonal, and rigged in the largest buyers' favor.

But no longer. In the information economy, commodities are mostly the province of low-wage countries. To survive the global meatgrinder, sellers have customized to the nth degree. Distinctive products and services build greater loyalty among end users— begetting tighter requirements on the buyer's side, and a narrower supply base. Deals are more complex and executed over longer periods. They're more likely to include issues that can't be fully factored into the initial terms. A negotiation over a design-build construction project or a byzantine outsourcing arrangement has more moving parts than an order for x grosses of felt tip pens.

Standardization is passé. Where young people once chose between Keds and PF Flyers, Nike now sells literally thousands of models of sneakers. Supply chains rely on customized inputs for parts, machinery, even outsourced production. The lowly spark-plug has evolved into a marvel of customization, geared to a gamut of compression ratios, chamber temperatures, timing specifications, firing gaps, and so on. The imperative to be *unique* inspires far-flung, exclusive associations. A Chevy Le Mans might be designed by one team in Italy, engineered by another in Germany, and manufactured by a third in Sweden or Japan.

Our point is that customized production has changed how we negotiate. Yesterday's purchasing heads are now "sourcing directors" or retail "category managers." It's no longer enough to solicit three bids and pick the lowest price. Now they're on the hook to develop strategic sourcing initiatives to boost quality and simultaneously drive down costs. New-era buyers begin by hunting for reliable suppliers with a track record of continuous improvement. When they find one, the ensuing parley goes lightyears beyond the price haggles of old. It's a mercurial climate, and companies often enter negotiations flying blind. The software that seemed ideal may in fact be suboptimal. An alternate version with extra features just might catapult your business to a whole new level—but only if you ask the right question. Dealmaking is no long linear. It's less about setting rigid criteria and more about exploring the realm of unknown possibilities.

Creative negotiators come armed with a diverse skill set, an agile mindset, a creative and collaborative outlook. They need to be detectives, debaters, strategic thinkers—even students of behavioral economics. They're expected to perform at a higher level than ever before.

The stakes are higher, too. Fierce offshore competition has narrowed everyone's margin of error. It's no longer enough to do everything right in product development, marketing, and production. If a company fails to harvest its good work at the bargaining table, those hard-won advantages drain away. Getting a better price is not just about beating the seller out of a few extra bucks to look good to your boss—it's a matter of survival. If the seller has flexibility, and your cost of acquisition is inflated, your company could find itself at a critical disadvantage to a competitor with a more aggressive purchasing team.

In business, as in life, much of your success depends on the agreements you make. Creative negotiating can have an outsize impact on individual careers, team performance, bottom-line results, and an organization's future:

- Salespeople close more profitable deals and build customer loyalty.

- Supply chain managers make better buys, generate savings, and strengthen vendor relations.

- Project managers run smoother, more profitable projects, delivering on time and under budget.

- Senior leaders enlist stronger commitment to milestones and objectives, promoting enhanced team member performance.

- Success breeds success—as performance improves, confidence and satisfaction soar.

Threats and Transformation

How else has negotiating changed? Let us count the ways:

1. **Price is no longer king.** At a recent seminar with a top metrology company (the people who measure auto parts with super-fine engineering tolerances), a salesperson told us, "We're the highest-priced firm out there. If we go out and just sell our product, we're dead—we won't make any sales. We've got to be selling solutions." Then there was the client we'd assumed was a coal company, until they corrected us: "We're an *energy solutions provider.*" The best price is no longer a deal's sine qua non. It makes little sense to get a rock-bottom number for software if you end up paying through the nose for training and customizing, plus next year's indispensable upgrade.

2. **Nearly everything's on the table.** There's vastly more headroom for both sides—more flexible pricing, and far more

opportunities to expand a deal. In the digital age, the cost curve of specialized products has plummeted. Which capabilities does the customer want optimized? How much technical support will be included? When every contract is a la carte, there's far more potential for creative problem-solving.

3. **Collaborative dealmaking is in vogue.** Newtonian physics seemed to work just fine until Rutherford and Einstein discovered subatomic particles: enter quantum mechanics. In contemporary business dealings, as negotiators delve more deeply into the finer details, the limitations of haggling have grown more apparent. It might seem paradoxical, but macrocompetitive forces are forcing negotiators to work harder at working with the other side.

4. **Back in 2007, Walmart changed its slogan from "Always low prices" to "Save Money. Live Better."** In 2017, it moved to retire its fabled price match program. Against rising competition from Amazon and eBay, Walmart realized it was no longer enough to refuse to be undersold—for a brick-and-mortar behemoth, it probably wasn't even possible. The company turned on a dime to enlist manufacturers for help in stocking higher-value products, the better to meet customer needs. To nourish those alliances, a somewhat kinder, gentler Walmart was forced to change the way they negotiated. (When you're beating the stuffing out of your suppliers, they're generally less inclined to collaborate.)

5. **Disruption is the rule, not the exception.** Companies worry less these days about a known rival underpricing them and more about the next existential threat from out of nowhere. A Chinese firm may emerge with a similar product at half the price. A new technology may render your keystone product obsolete. Kodak never saw the smartphone coming, and neither did BlackBerry. Uber and Airbnb have upended whole sectors; ditto for the Toyota Prius and the Tesla. Either we adapt or we leave the field. As W. Edwards Deming once said, "It is not necessary to change. Survival is not

mandatory."[1] Richard Branson couldn't agree more: "A company that stands still will soon be forgotten."[2]

The most successful businesses are constantly *looking*—not only behind them, at established competitors, but also ahead, to where the trailblazers are charging. Creative negotiators carve out uncontested market space with a blue ocean strategy. They leapfrog the competition with transformative deals.

Only skilled and savvy dealmakers can survive in the current environment. Only bold and inventive ones will grow. In a time of profound uncertainty, where organizations must adapt just to stay in the game, creative negotiating can make all the difference.

The Old Gold Standard

In 1968, an aerospace dealmaker named Chester "Chet" Karrass left the Howard Hughes Corporation to launch an eponymous company and a new-breed seminar program: Effective Negotiating. Soon it became the late century's gold standard. Chet came along at a time when business was highly structured, specialized, and commoditized. Variables were few. A buyer solicited bids to get the lowest possible price. Sellers scrambled to counter. Neither side had much room to maneuver.

Chet's big idea was that negotiators had more power than they realized. In fact, depending on the situation, they had a multitude of powers: the power of legitimacy, the power of leverage, the power of time and work, the power of knowledge. You simply had to spot them and then use them to your advantage. For most people, that was a revelation.

The Karrass Way was a blunt instrument that gave no quarter. In Chet's view, negotiation was a ruthless contest between winners and losers. Winners were hard-nosed, unrelenting, and supremely skeptical of any ostensibly firm position taken by the other side. The cardinal rule was to wield your power with self-assurance, to bargain as aggressively as you could until your adversary backed off or wore down.

Karrass didn't invent hardball tactics. Out in the trenches, rough-and-ready dealmakers were slugging it out with similar ploys, consciously or not. But Chet carved out a new industry by distilling these ideas into a formal training curriculum for novice negotiators and more experienced practitioners alike. Frank Mobus and I encouraged our clients to challenge how things were always done "because everybody does it that way." We emboldened them to defy conventional wisdoms—assuming they had the right tools, a Karrass strong suit. The program was packed with practical tips that actually worked: bargaining at the atomic level. It opened a window on real-world buyers and sellers, including their real-life dialogue. And it returned amazing value to those who followed its advice in the field.

Frank wasn't yet thirty when Chet gave him free rein to strengthen the program and train a new generation of negotiators. They signed up two-thirds of the *Fortune* 500, including GE, GM, IBM, Microsoft, Exxon, and DuPont. Frank learned as much as he taught at those sessions. He gained insights into best practices and how they varied from industry to industry, country to country.

Climate Change

Much has changed since Karrass put out its shingle. Globalization has disrupted almost every business sector. The tech-era marketplace is more competitive than ever, yet also more intensely cooperative. Microsoft and Intel showed the way with their Wintel duopoly. T-Mobile partnered with Nokia to build a 5G network. Microsoft and Walmart entered a cloud services partnership in their two-front war with Amazon. Meanwhile, countless small companies are using Amazon to find untapped markets.

As Daniel Pink points out in *To Sell Is Human* (2013), we live and work in a time of unprecedented information parity. For buyers and sellers alike, search engines and social media have leveled the playing field. All that data in the public domain makes it considerably more difficult to bluff or game your way to an advantage.

In long-term business relationships, trust beats trickery. Caveat emptor can backfire, sometimes fatally.

When buyers have limitless needs and sellers an elastic array of assets, or vice versa, the challenge becomes how best to align them. Today's negotiators may need to examine guaranteed gross margin or quality control or a dozen other factors. They'll often consider joint advertising or joint technology or even joint project management. By and large, price-driven bargaining won't get them where they need to go.

The Karrass Way remains highly effective in one-off settings, as you'll see in the second section of this book. If Party A wants to buy a truck from Party B, the right bargaining skills will give one side an edge. But in strategic, relationship-based scenarios, negotiators need a more versatile toolkit. Tactical warfare takes a backseat to innovative problem-solving. Savvy bargaining is but a means to broader breakthroughs—to the creation of additional, previously hidden value.

Win-Win

In 1981, around the time Frank joined the Karrass organization, *Getting to Yes* became an international phenomenon. Written by Roger Fisher and William Ury of the Harvard Negotiation Project, it was a manifesto for "principled negotiation," a stark contrast to the tooth-and-nail doctrine we taught at Karrass.

Fisher and Ury revolutionized the field. Old assumptions were turned upside down. To get to *yes*, negotiators were urged to:

- Invent new options, *then* decide

- "Focus on interests, not positions"[3]

- Insist upon objective criteria

- Be easy on the people but tough on the problem.

These were sound ideas, each and every one of them. But bear in mind that Ury was trained as an anthropologist, while Fisher was a law professor who helped mediate the Camp David summit accords. Where diplomacy can muddle on (and off and on) for years, most business deals come attached with urgency and internal constraints. Say you're a seller who's just been outflanked by a competitor, or a buyer flailing to keep pace with an unanticipated surge in demand. You may find yourself under the gun to close *today*.

Compete While You Collaborate

Fisher and Ury had a blind spot. They overlooked a core element of any negotiation—namely, power. In *Getting to Yes*, self-interest is disparaged as the sand in the gears of nonadversarial bargaining. Conflict is painted as counterproductive, an unnecessary evil to be "managed" and "resolved" by an invisible hand: "*independent of the will of either side.*"[4] [Emphasis added.] In the magical land of *Getting to Yes*, two reasonable people lay their cards on the table, agree upon objective criteria, perceive their common interests—and, voila!

That's our issue with the Harvard guys: They throw out the leverage with the bathwater. For better or worse, power matters. While modern negotiating is clearly more collaborative than it used to be, you can't wash the competition out of it. Even as we strive to expand the pie, we're still reaching for a bigger slice. In real life, "win-win" is often WIN-win or even—if one side is *really* skillful—*WIN!*-win.

So where do we go from here? As we've noted, the Karrass Way may be your cudgel of choice in basic bargaining—to keep your company from taking a bath, if nothing else. But in more intricate, far-reaching deals, the old tools are like using chisels for microsurgery. There's a fair chance the patient—the deal—will die on the table.

The Harvard school's win-win can also work like a charm, assuming you have the luxury of time and a like-minded counterpart "to produce wise outcomes efficiently and amicably,"[5] as the coauthors phrased it. But applied too loosely, win-win can be insidiously subjective. If negotiators are desperate enough to close a deal, they might give away the store and still *feel* like they've won. (To be fair, Ury would acknowledge the importance of conflict in his later work, including *Getting Past No.*)

A Third Way

Our main point is this: *All negotiations are not the same.* They take different paths, with a range of inflection points—or veer from one path to another in unpredictable ways. You can win every concession and lose the future if you beat up the other side and jeopardize a key relationship. On the other hand, you might choose to get less from a deal today in exchange for a stable and more lucrative arrangement down the pike. Which is the real victory?

In the not-so-olden days, most people negotiated in one of two ways: conflict avoidance or antagonistic conflict. Either they caved in and sacrificed their interests, or they hammered the other side to do the same. Or maybe they mechanically split the difference, a more subtle form of avoidance. In any case, the process was uprooted before it could bear fruit.

The new landscape cries out for a different slant. In a world of customized solutions, negotiators need a mix of sharp-edged tactics and collaborative strategies. They need to be tough *and* creative, to get a good price while finding ways to add to the deal's overall value. Most of all, they need different negotiating skills for different situations.

Frank and I thought there could be a third way, a more imaginative way. Where people strived to see the opposition's side as well as their own. Where disagreements were catalysts, not obstacles. Where mutual discovery unearthed new and added value.

We have a name for that third way. We call it *creative conflict.* And its seed was planted at a modest fourth-generation family business.

Negotiating Your Profit

Frank Mobus Sr., my coauthor's father, was a lifelong paving contractor who somehow stayed afloat in a boom-and-bust marketplace. Though he never took a seminar on the subject, he attributed the firm's decades-long survival to its knack for making better deals. The company's founder, Frank's great-grandfather, had a motto: "When times are hard, bid the job at cost, and profit is everything you negotiate."

Then as now, construction was a tough way to make a living. When business was flush, Frank's father could set his price high and mostly get it. Then a new wave of owner-operators would elbow onto their turf . . . until the inevitable downturn. As jobs dried up, the newcomers lowballed one another until they busted: death by a thousand undercuts.

To save his company from tanking with them, Frank Sr. would press his subcontractors and suppliers to shave a few percentage points. Then he'd shore up his top line by charging a stiff—though not outlandish—premium on change orders. Since it's costly to switch prime contractors midstream, the local public works department invariably gave in and ponied up. You can find a similar dynamic in the aerospace industry (with its notorious cost overruns), the home improvement business, and just about everything in between. The further along a job progresses, the more leverage shifts to the seller.

As his father began to share the reins, young Frank learned that most deals were more fluid than might first appear. When he couldn't get his targeted concessions, he'd try to find some other angle to take out cost or add value. Once he responded to a request for proposal at a Southern California shopping mall. The job entailed paving eight driveways from the two roads into the mall, fourteen parking lots, two miles of sidewalks, and extensive landscaping. Frank bid $1.7 million. He was called in by the mall's project manager, an affable fellow named Carson with whom he'd worked before.

"Look, Frank, I like your proposal and I know you'll deliver," Carson began. "But I've got a problem. You came in way over our budget." When pressed to be more specific, he said, "I can't tell you exactly, but it's in the range of 25 percent."

Frank did the math in his head and saw that he was staring at a $425,000 haircut. "Come on, Carson, that's below my cost," he said. "There's no way I can do the job for that price, and I don't see how anyone else will, either."

And the manager said, "Well, there's a couple outfits that must be really hungry, because they're pricing it really close. I'm not saying they're the best contractors in SoCal, but they can get the job done. I'd rather go with you, but I need you to get closer."

Conflict is a double-edged sword. As a contractor, Frank had witnessed its destructive side: yelling matches, impasse, the blame game. But from early on, he saw its opportunities as well. When handled constructively, disagreements allowed fresh viewpoints to percolate and benefit both sides. In the case at hand, Frank's wheels started turning. He'd tailored his bid to meet the letter of the RFP's requirements. But now he asked Carson, "Why did you specify ten-foot-wide sidewalks?"

"We went by the width for the mall we opened last year in Brooklyn."

That's when Frank pointed out that Brooklyn malls need wider walks for their voluminous foot traffic: "But everyone goes to this mall by car. You could save at least $50,000 with six-foot walks."

"You know what, that makes a ton of sense," Carson said. "And while we're on the subject, why not pave them in macadam instead of concrete? I'm guessing that takes out another $40,000 in material costs."

Soon the two of them were riffing like jazz musicians. Frank agreed to trim his price in return for larger up-front progress payments. Carson volunteered that the mall's resident maintenance crew could handle most of the landscaping, which meant Frank could descope the work and save a bundle on a pricy subcontractor. In lieu of a large fountain in the heart of the mall, Frank proposed smaller water spouts, a budget-friendly alternative that would delight the shoppers' children.

By the time they'd finished red-penciling the RFP, they'd found more than $300,000 in cost cuts. Carson was close enough to his budget to sell Frank's bid to the mall's owners. And by ridding himself of the less profitable pieces of the project, Frank increased his margin to the point where the job made sense. It all boiled down to asking one simple, critical question: *What do they really need?* That was a lesson Frank never forgot.

A Quick Roadmap

In this first section of the book, we'll consider the ancient origins of the Mobus Negotiating Continuum. We'll hear from leading behavioral economists on the roots of conflict aversion, the clash between social and market norms, and the self-destructive forces that undermine our interests: the four horsemen of anxiety, frustration, anger, and revenge. In subsequent sections, we'll dive into the continuum's three modes in greater depth. Using real-life examples and dramatic enactments, we'll demonstrate how the right tactics, strategies, and mindset can lead you to success at the bargaining table and beyond.

Conflict is an inescapable part of life. All of us negotiate past differences every day. Our hope is that *Creative Conflict* will help you to do so with less tension, fewer regrets, greater satisfaction, and consistently more profitable results.

Summary

- The essence of negotiation is in our differences. Value derives from the gap between two parties' positions and from their overlapping assets and needs. Creative negotiators steer away from antagonistic conflict and its mind-numbing side effects, anger and fear. They tack into *creative* conflict, a sea of mutual trade-offs and thoughtful compromise that gives birth to something new and better.

- Win-win is a myth. No matter how harmonious a negotiation may seem on the surface, the competition never completely disappears. A more fitting term might be "Better for Both." How *much* better for one party or the other will hinge on the relative skill of the negotiators.

- Enemy number one is conflict aversion. When people are *avoiders, accepters,* or *rejecters*, positive outcomes are unlikely. We'll explain how to think like a negotiator by curbing emotions, suspending judgments, and inviting more ambitious possibilities.

- Negotiating can't be reduced to one-size-fits-all. A haggle at a Shanghai bazaar demands a very different skill set—and mindset—than dealing with a sole-source supplier in Chicago or Berlin. We'll look at those differences through the lens of the Mobus Negotiating Continuum and its three modes: bargaining, creative dealmaking, and relationship building.

2

The Mobus Negotiating Continuum

Negotiate derives from two Latin roots: *neg*, or "not," and *otium*, or "leisure." Put them together and you get *negotium*—or "not leisure," a definition that will resonate with anyone who finds negotiating stressful. The verb form is *negotiat-*, "done in the course of business." Which suggests—correctly, in our view—that negotiating lies at the heart of all business relationships.

In medieval France, traders and merchants were known as *negociants*. (The term is still used today for large-scale wine merchants who buy grapes or finished wines from several growers.) These early negotiators propelled the economies of their day. They were the dealers, the doers—the people who got things accomplished.

But the roots of negotiating reach back further yet. Exchanges within families or kinship groups hail from prehistoric times. (Wedding rings go back at least 6,000 years, to Egypt before the pharaohs.) Trading was linked to specific words and gestures. In some cultures, negotiators staged ritual dances in the run-up to an agreement, advancing and retreating to anticipate the give and take of bargaining. Later they'd mark the deal's completion with another ritual—a handshake, a peace pipe, an initialed piece of paper.

The Great Unknown

Commercial trade goes back untold millennia, long before written records. Seashells dating from 40,000 BCE have surfaced thousands of miles from any shore. Paleoanthropologists believe they were an early currency. Though shells were eventually replaced by cattle or pieces of silver or Bitcoin, the core elements of transacting have stayed mostly constant: discovery, concession-making, declarations of fairness, claims to trust. In prehistoric times, when clans or tribes were more insular, negotiating was casual and less tactical. But with the growth of empire and the proliferation of global trade routes, buying and selling were transformed. The course of commerce took a radical turn. What changed?

We began dealing routinely with people we didn't know.

It's one thing to make a swap with your son-in-law or even your first cousin's uncle by marriage, where both sides are bound by family ties and community mores. It's another to stake your future—your possessions, your reputation, your ability to thrive (or survive)—on someone you've never met. As the world became a more nervous and uncertain place, trade followed suit. It wasn't just the quality of your barley or your goats that determined how you'd fare in a deal. It was how adroitly you traversed the precarious terrain of language and body language, of cultural norms and social cues, of concessions and hard lines. And most of all: of when to fear and when to trust.

These adaptations were universal to human societies. To this day, they define—or disrupt—our interactions with people we know, and even more so with those we don't. They guide what we call *creative negotiating*. What are the hallmarks of this process?

It is more than an economic activity. On the one hand, negotiating is an objective process, a trade of goods or services. On the other, it moves through the subjective medium of human communication, with a high risk for mistakes or misinterpretation.

It sets off our fear of the unknown. When you don't know the other party, it's fair to wonder how they might act or react—or what they might try to take from you. *Stranger danger* may be the stuff of irrational panic and xenophobia, but it's not without a certain crude logic. It's why so many people put off or resist negotiating and why rational judgment can get jettisoned along the way.

Negotiations are fluid, not fixed. Assuming we don't strangle the process or bail out prematurely, a seemingly cut-and-dried interaction can blossom into a journey of discovery and even a long-term relationship. To reap extra value from a deal, negotiators must adapt to the road's twists and turns. Only by hazarding the unexpected can we achieve a surprising success.

Over the millennia, cultures developed distinct gradations of social proximity and knowledge. Groups or individuals we didn't know, or knew only slightly or indirectly, posed an existential threat. Our response took one of three forms:

- **Suspicious self-defense.** You don't like them and believe you have reason to distrust them.

- **Guarded exploration.** You're not sure how much you like them but want to find out how far you can trust them.

- **Open-handed welcome.** You estimate that the reward outweighs the risk and give them every chance to earn your confidence.

These outlooks were not fixed for all time; rather, they were adapted to changing circumstances. Strangers evolved into friends, acquaintances became rivals or even enemies. The Mobus Negotiating Continuum grew out of this fluid behavioral spectrum. From our own first-hand experience, we knew that all negotiations were not the same. There were a multitude of variables: the size of the contract, the industry's norms, the other side's personality or track record. It seemed only logical that different sorts of negotiations called for different tactics, strategies, and skill sets. And so we set out to explain them.

The Continuum

The Mobus Negotiating Continuum consists of three modes that reflect the relationship between buyer and seller.

- Bargaining is a zero-sum exercise to *capture* value, a purely distributive process. Competition is primary, though both sides must at minimum cooperate in trying to reach an agreement. Creative bargainers embark upon discovery to probe the other side's vulnerabilities and also to gain a clearer understanding of their own needs. Submodes range from simple price haggling to advanced bargaining, where broader issues beyond dollars are brought to the surface. More sophisticated bargainers build narratives to inflate the subjective value of what they're offering in the eyes of their counterparts. In traditional supply chain or account management dealings, advanced bargaining is usually the end game—if the principals get that far. But for creative negotiators, it may be only the beginning. By sliding to the right on the continuum, they open the door to bigger and better agreements.

  Crucial questions: How much flexibility does the other party have? And what do I *really* need out of this deal?

- Creative dealmaking *surfaces* extra value when bargaining alone cannot close the gap. While this mode requires more effort, it can also pay substantial dividends—clarifying issues, cutting through deadlocks, soothing destructive tension. The lead strategy is value mapping, a discovery pathway that allows both sides to gain more than they relinquish—in other words, to grow the value pie. In this middle mode of the continuum, competition and cooperation

FIGURE 2-1

The Mobus Negotiating Continuum

Bargaining   Creative   Relationship
                    dealmaking   building

sit more or less in equilibrium. Even as the two parties join together to make a more comprehensive arrangement, they keep pushing to get their share of any added returns.

Crucial questions: How can the deal be expanded? Are there hidden assets that could create new value for either side?

- **Relationship building aims to *optimize* value over time.** Organizations need allies to stay ahead of the market curve—and to watch their backs in fending off challengers. As suppliers move from order-as-needed items to more specialized, integrated solutions, buyers are induced to lock down long-term arrangements. The apex relationship is a long-term strategic alliance or partnership, where each side negotiates for the other as much as for itself. Since alliances live or die on mutual confidence, transparency and fair play are of the essence. But while cooperation is clearly primary, a candid airing of different perspectives helps keep the relationship on track and prevents slippage.

  Crucial questions: What resources can we tap to deepen our relationship? How well can we work together—not just on our honeymoon or when all is going well but over the long haul or when times get tough?

As you may have deduced by now, we've listed these modes in order of ascending creativity, from the formulaic to the more flexible. The further to the right you move along the continuum, the more complex the negotiation and the greater the value-adding opportunities. That's precisely where the impetus is today, the direction the future is trending—and, in our experience, where negotiators need the most help. But no one mode is universally better than another. In a limited deal for a commoditized product, basic price bargaining may be the best way to go. When there's no future to the exchange nor any call to broaden it, why spend time building a relationship or searching for common ground? To everything there is a season. There are times to get in and out of a negotiation as quickly as you can, if only for efficiency's sake.

We should add that the three modes aren't mutually exclusive. Many negotiations shift from one to the next, or overlap or oscillate among them. Bargainers draw on relationship skills to elicit information—and to keep disagreements from blowing up the deal. Conversely, bargaining skills are useful across the whole continuum. We've seen strategic partners resort to haggling over a thorny point of contention or when a breach of trust threatens the relationship. Assuming the issue gets resolved, they can reset the partnership to where it was before or raise it to an even higher level.

Finding the Right Chair

One helpful way to think about the continuum is to visualize a table. In bargaining, the two parties are seated on opposite sides. (Or if matters get *really* adversarial, on opposite ends). In creative dealmaking, they've moved to the same side of the table but at proverbial arm's length. In relationship building, they're in adjacent chairs. There's no daylight between them; they're as close as two organizations with joint interests can be.

As we've noted, relationship building holds the greatest potential for adding value. At the same time, we'd argue that the crucial passage lies between bargaining and creative dealmaking, the point of transition between one-sided and two-sided thinking.

FIGURE 2-2

Bargaining

FIGURE 2-3

Creative dealmaking

FIGURE 2-4

Relationship building

To elaborate, bargaining is geometrically oppositional. Each of the two parties is tethered to a fixed position at a far remove from the other. Hampered by their own blind spots, they find it difficult even to imagine what their counterpart might be perceiving. The other side might as well reside on the dark side of the moon.

In creative dealmaking, we see a qualitative change. The two sides now share a similar vantage point. Their perspectives are complementary, if not quite identical. It's the equivalent of binocular vision, the anatomical feature that lends us depth perception. In negotiating, that's a huge plus for discerning new opportunities or resolutions. As we take to working together, our subjective interaction changes as well. Friction ebbs. While protecting our immediate interests and stopping short of long-term commitments, we're eyeing the horizon for possibilities to expand the deal.

Creative dealmaking is the bridge between combat and collective problem-solving. It's where we pivot from distrust to empathy, to the effort to put ourselves in someone else's shoes.

For creative negotiators, the first order of business is deciding exactly where you should sit at the table. (Keep in mind that you can move your seat later.) Once you sense where you are on the continuum, you'll be ahead of the game—and most of the competition. Sure, you'll still need to defend yourself. It still matters not to overpay or undercharge. But equally vital is a broader view of the *process* of negotiating, or what we call *external clarity*. The more aware you are of the mode you're in and the direction you're heading, the more you'll trust your game plan and be able to follow through. You'll stay confident through any turbulence that comes your way. Not least, you'll be less apt to make costly emotional mistakes.

Negotiations are inherently unpredictable. No book can help you win every deal, or even close every deal. But we'll promise you this: once you commit to creative conflict, in all of its elastic two-sidedness, you'll vastly improve your chances for a better outcome.

You Can Lead a Bargainer to Water . . .

Just as toddlers learn to crawl before they walk, creative negotiators are advised to find a comfort zone in bargaining before tackling the more collaborative, complex modes. The truth is, the most productive and durable business relationships usually begin on the left side of the continuum, with a wrangle over price. Here's a cautionary tale about the peril of skipping steps.

Eva was a young graphic designer who'd just gotten a promotion at a midsized arts organization in New York. In her new capacity as department head, she was dealing with outside printers for marketing pieces and catalogs. After attending one of our public seminars, Eva came up to us gushing over how it had opened her eyes. She'd never imagined there were so many ways and opportunities to negotiate, she said.

A few weeks later, her company asked me to pay them a visit and check on how their people were applying the skills we'd taught. When I stopped by Eva's office, she pointed to her new shoes—a pair of snazzy blue slingbacks—and said proudly, "I got $35 off!"

"That's great," I said, "but how are you doing on the business front?"

"Well, I'm pretty excited about this minibrochure we're getting printed tomorrow."

"What does a piece like that cost?"

"I got a really good price from this terrific guy named Howie—$4,500."

"Tell me about the negotiation. What was his starting quote? How much did you get him to come down?"

Oh no, Eva said, she couldn't bargain with him, "He's my boss's favorite printer, and he does really good work."

My alarm bells went off. When people make someone a partner before the relationship warrants it, it usually costs them a lot of money. "Wait a second," I said. "Did you get any other bids?"

And Eva said, "Oh, I couldn't do that to Howie. I'd feel like I was insulting him—he's like family around here." I got the picture. Howie had even had Eva over to dinner to meet his wife and kids. He was apparently a charming guy and a terrific salesman.

I couldn't let this slide, "But how do you know it's a good deal?"

"Because Howie's giving me his special price."

Francis Bacon was right—knowledge is power. Eva lacked power because she had no idea how much business her company did with her new best friend. At my prodding, she checked with accounting and discovered it was a *lot* of business, around $300,000 a year. For a one-man band like Howie, that figured to be a third or more of his total revenue.

I said, "I think you've got a little leverage with this guy." I asked Eva to get two competitive quotes—something she'd never done before—and to get back to me by end of day. The first printer she called came in at $4,200. The second one, with no prompting, bid $3,900. Howie's price was "special," all right. Eva was paying a premium for the pleasure of doing business with him.

"Okay, here's what I want you to do," I said. "Call Howie and tell him the market for the job seems to be around $4,000. Then ask him if there's anything he can do for you."

Eva was frowning, "But what if he doesn't come down?"

"Then you can say, 'What if we split the difference?'"

"But what if he won't split it?"

"Then you tell him, 'Look, I just need you to take $100 off and we can go ahead with the job.' I guarantee you he'll come down that far. If he doesn't, *I'll* pay you the hundred dollars. But you've got to give it a shot."

Though I could tell that Eva was uncomfortable with the prospect of conflict with Howie, she agreed to give it a whirl. When we spoke the next day, she sounded pleased with herself. "Well, Howie's going to do the job."

"How much?"

"You won't believe it—$4,000!" It was a 15-second negotiation. Once the printer realized that Eva had done her homework, he was happy to meet the market rate and keep a big customer satisfied. By no longer treating Howie like some long-lost cousin, Eva saved her company five hundred bucks. Even better, I thought, she'd learned a lesson for a lifetime.

Six months later, I ran into her at a midtown coffeeshop. She reached into her briefcase and pulled out the organization's new annual report. Four colors, splashy graphics—a first-rate job, all around. "That's beautiful," I said. "What did it cost to print that baby?"

"About $45,000."

"Howie?"

"Yup."

"So tell me, how did the negotiation go? What was your target price? Where did you anchor? How much did you get him down?"

"Oh, I just took the price he gave me."

"Wait—you didn't try to bargain with him?"

"Uh, no." Everything we'd talked about had flown away.

While I'd tried my best as Eva's negotiation tutor, I was the one who learned the more lasting lesson. Yes, I'd helped her gain some external clarity about the process. But she still lacked *internal clarity* on why we resist negotiating in the first place. In the moment of truth, Eva gave in. Like so many businesspeople, men and women alike, she defaulted to her comfort zone. When their budget allows, buyers tend to give in to their reticence to challenge the seller's price. To relieve the tension of conflict, they let slip the rope and sacrifice their interests.

To sum up, creative negotiating is more than a set of color-by-number guidelines. It's a different way of thinking, a new way of looking at the world. The best strategies will go for naught without the correct mindset to deploy them . . . which is the focus of our next chapter.

Summary

- All negotiations are not the same. Depending on the relationship between buyer and seller and the nature of their business, they fall into one of three modes. Each of them involves distinctive tactics, strategies, skill sets, and mindsets. The further to the right we move on the Mobus Negotiating Continuum, the greater a deal's creative potential.

- Bargaining is a zero-sum contest to *capture* value, an arena where competition outweighs cooperation. Bargainers gain an edge by probing the other side's flexibility and better defining their own objective needs.

- Creative dealmaking surfaces *added* value. It looks to expand deals via exchanges of complementary concessions, matching each party's assets with the other's needs. Competition and cooperation are more or less in equilibrium.

- Relationship building *optimizes* value over the long haul. In its apex expression, a long-term strategic alliance, each side essentially negotiates for the other in light of their common interest.

While cooperation overrides competition, contending perspectives keep both sides honest and point them to expanded opportunities.

- It's critical to know the mode you're in and in which direction the negotiation is heading. But it's equally important to cultivate the proper mental model to put the skills you've learned into practice.

3

Mental Models

Look inside any organization and you'll find two types of people. *Insiders* are the lock-step loyalists—the types who go along to fit in, no matter the cost. *Outsiders* are the contrarians at the gate, the ones who revel in contention and never met a battle they wouldn't escalate. Despite their obvious differences, as David Brooks observed in *The New York Times*, insiders and outsiders share much in common.[1] Both see the world as black and white, all or nothing, on the bus or off. Both dwell in a state of defensiveness, rigidity, anxiety, and fear.

In negotiating, outsiders tend to be ferocious bargainers, ready to blow up the deal unless they win on every point. Back in the day, we knew a subcontractor named Mike, a rejecter par excellence. A cement mason by trade, Mike cared only about getting the best possible deal for himself: best price, best payment terms, best delivery schedule, best *everything*. Mike treated each transaction like a game of chicken—or war. It wasn't enough just to win; if the earth wasn't scorched, he was disappointed. One time we had a ringside seat and asked him if he might be coming on a little too strong.

Mike replied, "If you show any weakness, they'll walk all over you." Convinced that everyone was dead set on fleecing him, he went for the jugular every time. And since the other side usually *would* back off, he'd get his way and prevail.

Until he didn't. Until people got so frustrated that Mike's every relationship was ruptured. Though his masonry was superb, no one wanted to deal with him anymore—it just wasn't worth the stress and resentment when you feel like you've been taken. His own workmen jumped ship. Mike wound up with nothing, on the outside looking in. He'd pushed too hard for his own good. For bare-knuckled bargainers, it's a cautionary tale.

Among our management clients, however, the chief complaint is just the opposite. Here's what they tell us: "My people give in so easily. How can I get them to be tougher and stop leaving so much money on the table?" Or put another way, "How can we get people to *think* like negotiators?"

This isn't a simple question. Human beings are hard-wired to get along with others, dating back to our earliest ancestors on the African savannah, where unity was a matter of survival. To be shunned from the group was a death sentence, a primal fear. Ostracized outsiders stood little chance against a saber-toothed tiger.

Flash forward one or two million years, and we still feel compelled to conform. Peer pressure doesn't end with adolescence. In the workplace, collaborative virtues reign supreme. To move up the ladder, we need to show we can play well with others: with our boss, our peers, our direct reports. When colleagues roll their eyes at some rising star who's adept at using connections, they're missing the point. In today's business culture, *connecting* is paramount— to the point where it may squelch internal dissent, as we'll see in chapter 13. As a classic article in *Harvard Business Review* noted: "We do what we believe other group members want us to do. We say what we think other people want us to say."[2]

In external negotiations, the yearning for inclusion makes insiders reluctant to say *no* or to press for a little more. *Avoiders* like Eva from chapter 2 short-circuit conflict with a quick and eager *yes*. *Accepters* dutifully go through the motions of bargaining but buckle in the end game. Both are selling out their interests to take an inferior deal. Why does this matter? It's about keeping your company on top in the marketplace. If a more assertive competitor gains a pricing advantage, it means waving goodbye to your market share.

A big part of our job is to figure out *why* negotiators act the way they do, to diagnose problems and prescribe correctives. We've found some answers in behavioral economics, a modern mash-up of money matters and psychology. Classical eighteenth-century economics—think Adam Smith—declared that human beings were coldly rational, motivated strictly by self-interest and monetary gain. Though this notion of *homo economicus* had remarkable staying power, it's been well debunked of late. Nobel laureate Richard Thaler reminds us that human behavior is a complex phenomenon. We're driven by more than the balance sheet—by fear and our sense of fairness, by our caring for others and anxiety over how they might perceive us. Thaler calls them "supposedly irrelevant factors" that actually "matter a lot."[3]

Thaler's argument applies in spades to the subject of this book. Online auctions aside, negotiations don't proceed between black boxes. They involve flesh-and-blood people, with all of our feelings, distractions, and mixed motives. In bargaining, in particular, a host of subjective factors color our sense of *value*, what we think we need or are willing to concede. In the tension of the moment, we can lose sight of the fact that the people on the other side of the table are human beings—that they're prone to careful analysis and dubious choices, iron discipline and wild impulses, cool logic and hot emotion.

In other words, they're a lot like us.

More than anything, behavioral economics explains the yawning gap between what you'd expect rational people to do and how they really act. Now let's turn to a few of the field's landmark ideas and how they might apply to creative negotiating.

Confusion Is Normal

As Daniel Ariely points out in *Predictably Irrational,* "we live simultaneously in two different worlds," the transactional world of business and the warm and fuzzy world of human interaction. The first is commanded by *market norms*, where we expect to get what we pay for. The second is governed by *social norms*, the land of community and friendship, where people do favors with no strings attached. Our problems start when we mix up the two.

Ariely imagines a case where a son-in-law commits a flagrant faux pas by injecting market norms into a social setting:

> Gazing fondly across the table at your mother-in-law, you rise to your feet and pull out your wallet. "Mom, for all the love you've put into this, how much do I owe you?" you say sincerely. As silence descends on the gathering, you wave a handful of bills. "Do you think three hundred dollars will do it? No, wait, I should give you four hundred!"[4]

While this breach of etiquette might seem outlandish, negotiators make comparable mistakes all the time, except in reverse. Like Eva, they misapply social norms to a market milieu. Over a friendly drink (or two), a buyer might blurt out to a seller, "Am I glad you bid on this! Not only is your product terrific, but you're the only ones who can meet our delivery date!" Why would anyone share such sensitive information? Because we're conditioned to be generous with our friends. By tangling his norms, the buyer has squandered all leverage.

Not for nothing are we known as social animals. We live most of our lives in society, not the market. We value social virtues: kindness, collegiality, self-sacrifice. Negotiating is counterintuitive because our social norms steer us toward conformity, if not timidity. At our two-day seminars, we'd close day 1 with a homework assignment: go out into the real world, challenge an ostensibly firm price, and report back the next day. It could be anything—a free dessert at dinner that evening, a 10 percent discount on a chardonnay at the liquor store, a few dollars off a pair of jeans at the mall. To their surprise, more than half of those who asked for a better deal received one. But here was the limiting factor: over the years, fewer than one of four people could get up the nerve to ask. (And ours was a cohort with a professional stake in negotiating!) Servers and salespeople are trained to be friendly. When we request a discount, we're disagreeing with their offer. Who wants to let a new buddy down? Based on our informal experiment over the years, it's safe to say that the great majority would rather pay more than risk instigating conflict.

Negotiating is doubly tricky because it's a hybrid animal, strictly business yet also up close and personal. It's not always clear where the socializing leaves off and business begins. You meet up with the other person and chat about sports or hobbies to get to know each other better. (Salespeople tend to excel at small talk, a time-honored device to get customers to let down their guard.) By the time you drift into the negotiation proper, your competitive edge is dulled.

We're not telling you to be unfriendly. People like doing business with likable people. In fact, you'll generally extract larger and easier concessions after establishing a rapport. But in bargaining, particularly between two unfamiliar parties, the market rules. Be affable, by all means. Just don't move so far inside their tent that you can no longer assert yourself or say no to their demands.

As we move to the right along the continuum, where relationships are more established, social norms play a progressively larger role. But remember the old adage: the toughest negotiations are with friends. As we've noted, the competition never entirely goes away, even when it's humming quietly in the background.

Slow and Steady

Like Richard Thaler, Daniel Kahneman won the Nobel Prize for economics—an impressive feat for a psychologist who never took an economics course in college. Kahneman's signature work, *Thinking, Fast and Slow* (2013),[5] forever changed our assumptions about the choices people make. The book's title refers to the two mechanisms warring for dominance inside our heads: our *automatic* system, home to intuition, gut feelings, and snap judgments; and our *reflective* system, our more logical and deliberate side.

The automatic system is involuntary and effortless—it's our default mechanism. As Kahneman points out, we routinely go on autopilot to add simple sums, drive on empty roads, or register concern on a friend's face. It would be exhausting to live without it. But left to its own devices, the automatic system is apt to be reckless and impulsive. It's gullible and overconfident and riddled with biases. When we negotiate, we might automatically smile and nod our assent to please the other side. Or, alternatively, we might erupt at their gall in disagreeing with our ideas. (And we *know* those ideas are correct—we came up with them!) Our automatic system focuses so narrowly and subjectively on the immediate conflict that it shuts down our ability to rethink the deal in a broader way.

That's where the reflective system comes in. While we can't rid ourselves of emotions (and we're not suggesting you try), we can consciously work to contain them. We can avoid hasty reactions that needlessly raise the stakes—where a difference over money, say, escalates into a harsh conflict over status or autonomy. If the other side acts in a hostile manner, as we'll see in the next chapter, it may be a tactic and nothing more. In response, you can be profitably tactical, as well—but only if you keep your wits about you and your automatic system under wraps. This is especially critical when communications and negotiations are virtual. Over the phone or on a video platform, the other side's body language or facial expressions are often MIA. Signals can be misconstrued. Which makes it even more important to move slowly and steadily, without haste or overreaction.

When the other party's hostility is unremitting, it can help to slow things down with a reflective response, a staple technique for both bargaining and creative dealmaking. Your decisions won't always be perfect, but pausing to think them over will likely lead to better choices. Here's a quick example:

Buyer: How about if we split the difference?

Seller #1: (*Eagerly.*) Sure, you've got a deal!

Seller #2: (*Angrily.*) Are you crazy? Forget it!

Seller #3: (*Pulls out her phone and takes 20 seconds to tap out a calculation.*) I'm sorry, but I don't think that quite works for us. Let me talk to my boss and get back to you.

By decelerating the process and buying a bit of time, seller #3 disabled her automatic system and regained her composure. It doesn't even matter whether she used her phone for real or for show. Alternately, she might have taken a bathroom break, or a deep breath, or counted slowly to ten. The point is to give our reflective system—our cooler and more collected but slower system—a chance to activate.

Another illustration: An account manager is negotiating the sale of 200,000 handsets with a sourcing manager at a telecommunications company. The seller's cost is $48 per unit. An intense session has driven his asking price down to $50—the number he'd set as his walk-away price going in. The buyer has dug in at $49. Neither side is budging. Finally the buyer says, "All right, you drive a hard bargain. Let's do it at $49.75 and call it a deal."

The seller says, "I told you, I can't take anything less than $50."

"Come on," the buyer says, "be reasonable. It's twenty-five cents! Are you going to sink this sale over a lousy quarter?"

It's late, and the account manager is tired and hungry. His automatic system is on full blast: *The guy's got a point, it's just a quarter! Let's close and go home!* He nods his head, mumbles his assent, and slumps in his chair with fatigue. It's only when he gets to the parking lot that his reflective system kicks in and does the math. That lousy quarter will cost the seller's company $50,000, a big chunk of the gross profit he'd promised his boss. The moral of the story? Our automatic system is less than brilliant at quantifying values.

Allow us to add one qualification to the above. With enough repetitions, as concert pianists and neurosurgeons can attest, the reflective can become automatic. As you gain hands-on experience and polish your skills, your negotiating instincts will become less risky and more reliable.

Giving and Getting

In his modern classic *Give and Take* (2014), Adam Grant lays out the three reciprocation styles found in the workplace:

- *Takers* see the world as a hypercompetitive rat race. Since they assume that no one else will look out for them, they place their own interests first and last. They may choose to help others strategically but only when the benefit seems to exceed the cost.

- *Matchers* operate tit for tat. When people do them a favor, they repay in kind—no more, no less. When they help someone, they expect the same in return. Think of them as market norms incarnate.

- *Givers* focus on others more than on themselves. They pay close attention to what people need from them, whether it's time or ideas or mentorship. A rarity in the workplace, according to Grant, their style is more typical of the way we treat family and friends.[6]

In any given field, you'll find givers near the tops of the charts. As they pay it forward, according to a number of studies, givers make for more efficient engineers or higher-grossing salespeople than either takers or matchers. Grant proposes that these high performers are strategic in the choices they make and the limits they set. Most of all, they've learned how to get help when they need it; they're skilled at receiving as well as giving. "Successful givers are every bit as ambitious as takers and matchers," Grant writes. "They simply have a different way of pursuing their goals."[7]

Yet the same research found a significant set of givers clumped at the opposite end of the bell curve. They're the least productive workers—the failures, at least in the eyes of their peers. What are they doing wrong? According to Grant, these hapless pure givers find it awkward to solicit favors or assistance. They give and give until the well runs dry. We knew a young travel agent who was bright and hard-working but consistently fell short on his sales numbers. After a ten-minute talk, we figured out his problem. He was compulsively generous with prospective clients, gifting them shrewd free advice . . . which they took to book online, to save themselves a commission. As a result, both the agent and his agency were suffering.

What does any of this have to do with negotiating? Quite a lot, in fact. Grant's reciprocation models map neatly to our negotiating continuum. Zero-sum bargainers are necessarily takers;

their gain is the other side's pain. Creative dealmakers are matchers, calibrating fair exchanges to benefit both sides. Relationship
builders are predominantly givers, willing to help the other party
even to their own short-term disadvantage.

The equation isn't absolute. It's possible to give constructively—
within limits—at any point on the continuum. The most one-
dimensional price haggle requires the gift of your time and
energy to make it through the process. Conversely, indiscriminate
handouts can be detrimental, even between strategic partners. In
short, it's important to distinguish between passive giving and
negotiated giving. Passive givers are giving *in* to avoid conflict, en
route to stunted deals and lowered expectations. Negotiating givers are more intentional in their generosity. While not chained to
explicit quid pro quos, they stay focused on their long-term goals.

We believe that anyone can become a successful negotiating
giver—if they have the right mindset.

Mental Modeling

Formed early in life, our mental models frame our behavior, especially in times of stress. If our model is built around anger or
suspicion, our actions follow in kind. But our mental models don't
have to be our destiny. Creative negotiating begins with a re-
oriented mindset—a willingness to think against the grain, out of
the box, sometimes outside your comfort zone. We're not suggesting a personality or character makeover—it's more about coming
to grips with who you are and tweaking your performance style
accordingly. Negotiating enlists our *outer* selves more than the
elusive inner ones, which are more resistant to change. Adam
Grant offers excellent advice in this regard: "Pay attention to how
we present ourselves to others, and then strive to be the people we
claim to be." Aim for "sincerity," he advises, rather than "authen-
ticity."[8] Positive mental modeling is constructed upon a flexible
framework for engaging the world.

Both Eva and Mike were trapped by negative, rigid, one-
dimensional mental models. Eva obsessed over what the other

person might think of her; Mike worried about how that other person might harm him. It's a matter of picking your poison—conflict avoidance or antagonistic conflict. Some people bounce between the two. They mute their differences to stave off conflict as long as they can, until they're so fed up that they lose their temper and explode.

According to neuroscience, our hair-trigger automatic system is steeped in evolution. It's a prehistoric mechanism embedded in the amygdalae, a pair of almond-shaped neuron clusters deep inside our mammalian limbic brain. When our forebears came under siege, the amygdalae boosted blood flow to the muscles in their extremities, with a dash of adrenaline thrown in for extra strength and speed. This enabled them to repel an invading clan or escape a woolly mammoth—fight or flight.

But there's a catch. Our ancient stress response shunts blood flow and oxygen *away* from the frontal lobes of our cerebral cortex, our executive reasoning center. Unless we consciously intervene, the emotional brain trumps the more recently evolved rational brain. When we feel threatened and capitulate to stress, it jams our capacity for flexible, resourceful thinking. To engage in creative conflict, we need to tamp down our amygdalae and restore our cerebral cortex to its rightful authority.

Your Front Foot

If you've ever watched a professional soccer game, you may have noticed a common trait of successful teams. Whether on offense or defense, they're always looking to advance—not plunging ahead recklessly, but playing with a balanced attack or counter. Star players stand out for their body language as much as their ball skills. They radiate a forward-leaning confidence. We call it *staying on your front foot.*

Negotiating on your front foot means raising your aspirations for the outcome. As Stephen M. R. Covey wrote in *The Speed of Trust* (2008): "Having a mind-set of expecting to win increases our odds of winning. It helps us get better results. And better results help us increase our credibility and self-confidence, which leads to more positive self-expectancy, and then more winning—and the upward cycle continues."[9] It's a self-directed version of the Pygmalion effect. The side that sets higher expectations usually comes out on top in the deal.

Front-foot negotiators are constructively aggressive. Since they're well prepared going in, they rarely get caught flat-footed or rocked back on their heels. Rather than conceding too quickly, they keep asserting their interests. Thinking like a negotiator begins as soon as you walk through the door. It's an air of confidence and control that's apparent in your face, your voice, your posture. One of the best negotiators we ever met was a Karrass veteran named Mel Klayman. At crunch time, when you could feel the nervousness all around, Mel would tilt forward in his seat with a half-smile on his face. You could almost hear him thinking: *Okay, the game's on—this is going to be fun.* His easy self-assurance unnerved the other side and kept his own fight-or-flight impulses at bay. While others were stressed, Mel was having fun.

Here's a terrific mindset for negotiators: *They can't do this deal without me.* It validates your position, keeps you on your front foot. It's especially helpful for salespeople, since buyers generally have more options and therefore hold the high ground. A favorite buyer attack line goes something like this, "Your competition is offering the same thing you are, only cheaper." The salesperson should reflect: *If the competition is so great, why aren't they using them already? Why did they ask me to come in and make my presentation?* In fact, there's a good reason you've been invited to the party, and it's not philanthropy on the buyer's part. As we'll illustrate later on, *both* sides are under pressure in every deal. Keep that in mind, and you'll find it easier to stay on your front foot.

Living with Ambiguity

In the 1950s, a psychologist named J. P. Guilford devised a test for creativity. It was a way to gauge *divergent thinking*, the ability to imagine a multitude of possible approaches and solutions to a single problem. Divergent thinkers were spontaneous, persistent, and endlessly inquisitive.[10] Unlike binary thinkers (on or off, my way or the highway), they were highly flexible. Unlike convergent thinkers, they were more intrigued by an abundance of nonlinear connections than by one correct answer.

Divergent thinking is the nub of creative conflict. As in literature or sculpture, there's no predetermined solution in negotiating, no absolutely perfect price. Negotiations exist precisely because there are *many* solutions, an array of possible agreements between buyers and sellers, none more intrinsically correct than another.[11] Creative negotiators are willing to live for long stretches in ambiguity, in a state of not knowing. They're able to keep contending ideas in tension without prematurely landing on either one. Or as Kahneman puts it, they "maintain incompatible possibilities at the same time."[12]

It's not entirely natural to think this way. Most people are uneasy with ambiguity because they equate it with danger.[13] In conflicting situations, their automatic systems take over. They get stuck inside their own heads in partisan default mode. They push for certainty and closure, even if the outcome might not be so wonderful. They're not thinking like negotiators.

But for those who can stay the two-sided course, who prevail in finding ways to reconcile opposing ideas, there's a rich reward. It's a clear-sighted vision of who you are, where you're headed, and how you're going to get there.

The Edge of the Inside

Divergent thinkers are neither insiders nor outsiders, they find a middle ground. David Brooks calls it "the edge of the inside,"[14] a phrase he borrowed from a Franciscan friar named Richard Rohr. When people live at the center of things, Rohr wrote, we're apt to "confuse the essentials with the non-essentials." And he went on:

> When you live on the edge of anything . . . you are in a very auspicious and advantageous position. . . . Not an outsider throwing rocks, not a comfortable insider who defends the

status quo, but one who lives precariously with two perspectives held tightly together—the faithful insider and the
critical outsider at the same time.[15]

To deal on the edge of the inside is an exercise in humility. As
Rohr says, "Thinking we have all the answers" will make us "arrogant, falsely self-assured, and closed down as a person. . . . Answers
are a plus in the technical and practical world, but a liability in the
world of philosophy, art, poetry, invention, enterprise."[16]

We'd submit that negotiating belongs to that second world; it's
more art than engineering. Creative negotiators don't leap to con-
clusions. They suspend judgments and ask loads of questions—
they're curious, above all. Rather than pulling up the drawbridge
and hiding behind the ramparts of certainty, they're willing to
open up and listen to what the other person has to say, regardless of whether they'll agree with it at the end. In standing on the
edge of the inside, they're saying: *This is my proposal, and I feel
strongly about it, but I'm willing to acknowledge that you might
have a better one.*

As we move right on the continuum, to creative dealmaking and
relationship building, a divergent approach is essential. Empathy
is hard work, but it pays to make the effort. Even when our idea *is*
better, it's probably less than perfect. We all have blind spots, after
all. There's a lot to be gained from the wisdom of crowds, even a
crowd of two. By engaging in a freewheeling clash of ideas, negotiators on the edge gain precious clarity. They break through to solutions that neither party might have seen on its own.

Even in one-off bargaining, a sea of fierce partisanship, an open
mind is invaluable. When we take the time and trouble to discover
the other side's vulnerabilities, we accrue leverage for a better
price. When we invite them to poke holes in our position, we can
shore up our weaknesses and make ourselves less assailable in the
conflict to come. By escaping the whirlpool of one-sidedness, we
free the bargaining process of much of its destructive tension.

One purpose of this book is to help people bargain harder and
smarter and more courageously, with less fear and loathing. That's
the focus of our next section.

Summary

- Negotiating is a hybrid process, a mix of market and social norms.

- Avoiders, accepters, and rejecters are their own worst enemies. By short-circuiting creative conflict, they sell their own interests short.

- While emotions can't be kept out of a negotiation, they need to be contained. When we slow things down, we allow our reflective system to kick in and overcome our fears, anxieties, and anger.

- Creative negotiators are divergent thinkers. They believe that every problem has a broad range of solutions.

- The sweet spot for creative conflict is the edge of the inside. It's the space where we affirm our own idea with confidence but stay open to the possibility that someone might have a better one.

Part Two

THE GAMESMAN

(BARGAINING)

Avoiding   Haggling   Broadening
                                    the deal

4

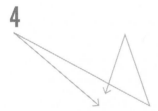

Overcoming Our Fears

Bargaining is the oldest form of negotiating, the mode where most deals start and many of them end. It's no place for the faint of heart. Since we're splitting a fixed and predetermined pot, my gain is your loss and your gain is my cost. Both sides are asking themselves, *How can I get what I want while giving up as little as possible?* That's a sure recipe for conflict. And since conflict is threatening, people tend to skew to one of two poles: Eva's yin or Mike's yang, passive acceptance or hostile intimidation. Neither leads to satisfying outcomes.

The elusive sweet spot lies somewhere in between. Whether it's simple haggling (a.k.a. price pushing) or a more complex deal, creative bargainers take a tough but balanced stance. They stand by their convictions without needlessly insulting the other party. They work to gauge the other side's flexibility and to clarify their own requirements. When conditions allow, they'll shift to the right on the continuum, toward creative dealmaking. But even when a broader deal doesn't seem to be in the cards, the most rudimentary one-time haggles contain a creative element. There's a craft to enhancing the perceived value of your offer. It takes finesse to probe what you might get in exchange, and whether it's what you really need.

Bargaining is difficult because people get locked into their positions and offended when they're challenged. Both sides place a *subjective value* on what they're bringing to the deal. When they clash over price, those values become inflated. The gap between the two parties swells. A request for some piddling sum or trivial concessions sets off a rush of negative emotion. Our tunnel vision narrows until we can barely see. As William Anton points out, "When faced with stress, we tend to increase the intensity, frequency and duration of habitual responses."[1]

Antagonistic conflict is the nemesis of creativity. As positions harden, we feel cornered. We're so absorbed by the conflict that we lose sight of possibilities for a more lucrative deal. One reason that so many people negotiate so poorly is that they feel trapped, even suffocated, by the process. The stress grows so intense that they'll rush to sign on the dotted line if only to escape it. One purpose of this chapter is to unpack these fears and phobias and show how they may be overcome.

Collaborative Conflict

In zero-sum bargaining, as we've noted, competition is front and center. The goal is to get a deal on the most favorable terms to your organization. Even so, competition isn't the whole enchilada. Deals run aground when the two sides lose sight of the *cooperative* side of the dialectic. No matter how cutthroat a transaction may seem, it cannot be resolved unless both parties agree to the following:

- There is a meaningful difference in our positions, and it's worth our while to try to hash it out.

- Until proven otherwise, we believe we have more to gain by reaching an agreement than by walking away.

- We'll help each other learn more about what we need.

Make no mistake: Bargaining is always adversarial. As long as we stay within this mode, we're vying for a bigger slice of a fixed pie. But when we take the time and trouble to *explain* their positions, we're giving the other party something more valuable than a price concession. By sharing information, even within tactical limits, we gain clarity about the other side's assets and our own deeper needs. Assuming we reach a deal, we've cooperated to create something (an agreement) out of nothing (two sides locked in opposition).

As a caveat, it's important to distinguish cooperation from capitulation. Eva-type accepters are every negotiator's fantasy: *I'd love to go up against somebody like that—I'd always get my way.* But beware: Someone who easily agrees may not be really agreeing. They may be nodding their head out of a get-along mental model, not because they stand behind the agreement. Down the road you may be in for disappointment. Maybe they'll resent you and change their mind before signing. Or maybe their organization will overrule them and replace them with somebody tougher. While conflict can be temporarily repressed, it can't be escaped. If it's swept under the carpet, it may rear its head when you least expect it, at significant cost.

The Myth of the Firm Price

The bane of business negotiators is the standard price, ostensibly set in stone. "It's our bottom-line number, there's nothing I can do about it," a seller will insist. Or, "You want a discount—are you kidding? This item is so hot that it's about to be sold under allocation." Or a buyer will shrug and say, "That's all we have in our budget—you can't get blood from a turnip."

With very rare exceptions, they're telling you less than the whole truth. Like hotel rack rates, firm prices are a tactic, no more and no less. Left unchallenged, the stated price is indeed what you'll be stuck with. It's up to you to carve out space to negotiate with strategies and tactics of your own.

There's nothing natural about firm prices. Over the many millennia of human commerce, they're a relatively new phenomenon— around three hundred years old in Europe, about half that in the United States. The Pennsylvania Quakers' "honest price" was institutionalized in 1874 by John Wanamaker, when he opened his eponymous department store in Philadelphia. A renowned innovator of the highest integrity, Wanamaker was the first retailer to offer money-back guarantees. He also invented the price tag: "A devout Christian, he believed that if everyone was equal before God, then everyone should be equal before price."[2] Before Wanamaker's, every purchase was open to a haggle. After Wanamaker's, set prices made buying and selling more uniform and efficient. They enabled discounts and holiday sales. But they also deprived proprietors and customers of a more artful, personal, satisfying way to arrive at the value of something on offer.

In today's transparent global economy, with so much data freely available online, negotiating opportunities abound like never before. Whether you're enlisting software talent by the hour or buying a living room set, all prices are open to question—even when the seller's complaining, "You're killing our margin!" There's no law that people have to make a profit. Cars are sold at a loss all the time. Recently a barrel of oil was priced at a *negative* $37.63. Sometimes it costs a seller more not to sell an item and have it clog their inventory than to write off a loss and move on.

Though we'll delve into bargaining strategies and tactics in more detail in the following two chapters, here are a few basic concepts with nigh-universal application:

> **Competitive leverage.** Never walk into a negotiation without options. One tried-and-true line: "I can get it cheaper elsewhere." Like most gambits, this one works better if you can back up your claim.

> **Timing.** Shoppers often check when the next sale is coming. What they forget to ask about is the date of the *last* sale. If it was relatively recent, you have every right to request the sale price. Or you might ask when a new model is coming in, laying the basis for a discount on the current model, which will soon be obsolete.

> **Take on higher authority.** Ask to speak to the salesperson's supervisor, who will likely have more latitude on pricing. Or invoke higher authority on your side—"I'd love to buy it, but my [spouse/boss] won't go for it at that price."

Be ready to walk out. If all else fails, don't be afraid to walk away. If the seller is able to make a larger concession, they'll entreat you to come back. If they don't, you can swallow a bit of pride and return anyway.

Are these stratagems guaranteed to get you a better deal? No, but you'll win more than you lose—and when you think about it, you have little to lose by trying. One thing is certain: Those who don't ask, don't get. In business-to-business negotiations, as we'll see, similar ploys can be used to great effect.

Why Bargaining Scares Us

Conflict provokes a muddle of emotions: frustration, anxiety, rage. But the most prevalent feeling is fear. People are afraid they'll be overmatched or outmaneuvered. They're intimidated by the game and unsure of its rules. At the extreme, there's a subjective sense of danger—*who knows where this could lead?* To wit, a T-shirt popular at gun shows pictures an AK-47 over this ominous text: *When negotiations fail.* At times bargaining seems no more than a thin veneer of civility over a deep well of mayhem, a brawl waiting to happen. We're not just talking about drug deals gone bad, where somebody literally starts shooting. How about the harmless fender-bender, where the drivers disagree about who's at fault and wind up in a shoving match, or worse? At a seminar debrief, two of our attendees started arguing over who'd insulted whom during the exercise. One of them growled, "Keep it up, keep it up, and I'll come over there and punch you right in the mouth!" He wasn't kidding.

Referencing the work of the psychologist Dolf Zillmann, Daniel Goleman explains:

> The universal trigger for anger is the sense of being endangered. Endangerment can be signaled not just by an outright physical threat but also, as is more often the case, *by a symbolic threat to self-esteem or dignity, being treated unjustly or rudely, being insulted or demeaned, being frustrated in pursuing an important goal.*[3]

Bargaining is a minefield of symbolic threats. Its undercurrent of violence stems from our generalized fear of conflict, a big reason why people leave money on the table. Either they're derailed by anger or intimidated into getting pushed around. Their expectations plummet. They reassess their targets and keep ratcheting them down. If the other side offers something even remotely acceptable, they'll jump on it: closure for its own sake. Unfortunately, they'll pay a stiff toll for our surrender. Not only will the outcome suffer in absolute terms, but they'll also have forfeited a chance at a broader solution to expand the deal.

Other fears are subtler but no less damaging to our interests:

- **Fear of failure.** Negotiating is unpredictable. Often the stakes are high, and a bad mistake at the bargaining table can damage an organization and even derail a career. While a great outcome may lead to a promotion, a blown deal can trigger an exile to the branch office. The quicksand is real. At the same time, the fear of failure can be self-fulfilling, especially when it stems from a "fixed mindset"[4]—the belief that how you perform is determined by who you are, your "fixed" characteristics. If you fail, you are perforce a failure—which sets you up to fail the next time.

- **Fear of losing.** A first cousin to fear of failure, this one's the product of a one-sided, partisan, win-lose mentality—a counterproductive obsession with results. You're so narrowly focused on your target price that settling for anything less (or more, if you're a buyer) means that you've lost the contest. As Richard Thaler and Cass Sunstein note in *Nudge*, losing something "makes you twice as miserable as gaining the same thing makes you happy."[5] Loss aversion stops stock market investors from buying the dips. It leads football coaches to punt on fourth down and a yard to go against all analytics to the contrary. When you're fixated on winning and unwilling to give an inch, your imagination shuts down. You may be arrogant, even bullying. You're effectively blind to the other side's pressures—notably, their own fear of losing.

- **Fear of being wrong.** Our ideas are like our children, to be cherished and defended. When people disagree, they're attacking our progeny. By extension, they're rejecting *us*—and what could be more insulting (or threatening) than that? To shield ourselves, we write off our critics as dishonest or obtuse. The pitfall is that no one is omniscient. Even when our idea is correct (or at least mostly correct), the other side's position may contain some useful kernels of truth.

- **Fear of seeming greedy.** Many of us shrink from forceful negotiating out of concern for how we'll be perceived. *Am I overstepping my bounds? Will the other side feel insulted if I imply they're overcharging? Will I lose their future business?* Most of all, we're protective of our self-image. As fair-minded people, we want only a fair price; asking for more can feel like cheating. The flaw in this reasoning is that pricing is largely subjective. When you're buying or selling in a complex market, a fair price cannot be determined in the abstract. The point of bargaining is to test the marketplace. If two sides negotiate creatively, what's fair will surface naturally, in good time.

False Certainty

People's fears notwithstanding, most business transactions entail very little raw conflict. The reality is that reluctant bargainers are paralyzed *before* the negotiating begins. When we dig into their apprehensions, here's what they tell us:

- The other side's holding all the cards.

- They'll shoot down my proposal, and I'll have nothing to counter with.

- I really need them, but they don't need me.

- It's going to be a train wreck—I just *know* I'm going to get killed on this deal.

These fears reflect two misconceptions. The first is the human inclination to catastrophize, to exaggerate every negative possibility. The second is a doomsday certainty about the outcome. But as we've noted, both parties have needs and pain points. (If the other side didn't need you, why would they bother to meet with you?) Avoiders like Eva dwell on their own weaknesses without pausing to consider the other side's duress. They fail to consider that their opposite number might be just as anxious and intimidated as they are, if not more so. Finally, the very essence of negotiating is *uncertainty*, since every deal contains a host of feasible solutions. If the outcome was preordained, you wouldn't be trading ideas in the first place.

Thinking like a negotiator means accepting uncertainty as part of the territory. It's like reading a spy novel. You can't be sure exactly how things will turn out at the end, and you know the journey will be nerve-racking at times, but you're excited by the possibilities and determined to see the story through. When bargainers avoid conflict, they never find out how far they can push for concessions. If they rush through the give-and-take, they may never discover their true needs.

Depending on the circumstances and the other party's temperament, a creative approach may be easier to prescribe than to execute. Bargaining can be frustrating when you're making no headway and don't much like the other side. It's tempting to give up and move on. One of our clients told us, "I've tried all your ideas and nothing's worked. I'm dealing with somebody who's like a stone wall. I don't want to waste more time. I just want to close the deal. There's nothing more I can do."

But here's what we'll tell you from first-hand experience: *There's almost always something more you can do.* Impasses are seldom permanent. Instead of giving up or giving in, you may need to aim *higher* while coming at the problem from a different angle. Sometimes that means finding a crack in the other side's armor to gain more leverage. Or you may pierce their resistance by broadening the deal beyond price.

Creative conflict contains one hard requirement: Don't be too quick to assume the game is over. Creative negotiators are steadfast. They explore every avenue, knowing that most will be dead ends. There's no telling in advance where an overlap of interests might be found. Just keep reminding yourself: *Even though this guy is acting like a jerk, I'm going to keep trying to figure out a deal that works for us—and maybe if I try long enough, he'll turn out not to be a jerk, after all.*

Emotional Detachment

In general, our negative feelings toward bargaining have less to do with the issues or the opposition and more with our unconscious mental models going in. The proof? Later on, after we've cooled off and achieved some emotional and physical distance, we invariably think of things we *could* have said to make a better deal.

The flip side of fear is anger, the fight that complements flight. When dealing with a bellicose adversary, or one who boomerangs between passivity and aggression, our automatic system will strain at the leash to react in kind. But assuming the ultimate goal is an agreement, battles of will have no winners. It's up to you to subdue your own ego and ire, your automatic responses—though it won't be easy. Anger, as Goleman says, "is the most seductive of the negative emotions. . . . Unlike sadness, anger is energizing, even exhilarating."[6]

Your reflective system is better equipped to see you through the storm. Above all, resist the urge to take an outburst personally and get sucked into antagonistic conflict. When the other side's amygdalae have overwhelmed their frontal lobes, it may have little or nothing to do with you. Consider what might be driving their behavior, then draw them into conversation. Don't contradict them. Instead, take the edge off their anger by asking open-ended questions. (*Why* and *how* are good places to start.) Keep your voice low and nonthreatening to diffuse the tension and lead them to listen more intently.

In the face of heated contention, the state to strive for is emotional detachment, or what Ury calls "going to the balcony."[7] No matter how stubborn or vehement the other side might seem in the moment, try to separate the person from the problem. Instead of saying "You're wrong!" or even "I disagree," you might ask: "What do you mean by that?" Or: "Help me out here, I'm confused." You're not rolling over; you're hearing the other person out. And if it turns out your argument was wrongheaded, isn't it better to find that out *before* the contract is signed?

Most people cling tightly to their ideas. Chet Karrass coined a great phrase: *forever for now.* I'm hearing where you stand right now, but now is not forever. As long as a deal is in play, positions are subject to revision. In fact, the pictures in people's heads are constantly changing. They may simply need more acceptance time to come around.

When the other side seems unyielding, rather than respond in kind, you might sit back and say to yourself, *That's their starting position. If we give the process a chance, the fuller story will emerge and maybe they'll be open to compromise.* Bargaining is dynamic. Today's line in the sand is erased by tomorrow's breeze. Tweak the emotional environment, and the most adamant positions will change. New ideas will supplant the old ones with equal conviction.

The point of creative conflict is to encourage contention without strangling the process. By tamping down the heat and stripping away the bluster, you'll gain a more accurate picture of the other side's reality, their strengths and vulnerabilities. What's more, an emotionally neutral state will help you strategize around what you've learned and reach a better outcome, the subject of our next chapter.

Summary

- In zero-sum bargaining, conflict is unavoidable. The trick is to avoid *antagonistic* conflict that overwhelms the creative quest for a more profitable deal.

- The most adversarial negotiations contain a cooperative element. It helps to keep in mind that both sides have more to gain by hashing out their differences than by killing the process.

- With rare exceptions, there's no such thing as a firm or fixed price or position. "Take it or leave it" is a tactic, no more and no less.

- Successful bargainers recognize and disarm their fears—of failure, of losing, of being wrong, of appearing greedy.

- The other side needs you as much as you need them or they wouldn't be talking to you in the first place.

- When a negotiation gets stuck and your counterpart seems immovable, don't presume you're at an impasse. They may simply need more acceptance time to come around to your point of view.

5

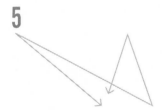

Bargaining Strategies

In the scene below, from the comedy classic *Monty Python's Life of Brian,* our hero is on the run from a phalanx of Roman soldiers.[1] He races into a crowded marketplace, spies a vendor's stall, and grabs an artificial beard—the perfect disguise. All he needs to do is make a deal for it.

Brian: How much, quick!

Harry the Haggler: Ah—twenty shekels.

B: Right. (*Slaps a coin on the counter.*)

HH: Wait a minute, we're supposed to haggle!

B: I haven't got time—

HH: Look at it. Feel the quality! That's none of your goat.

B: All right, I'll give you nineteen then.

HH: No, no, no, come on, haggle properly. This isn't worth nineteen.

B: You just said it was worth twenty!

HH: Oh dear, oh dear. Come on, haggle!

B: I'll give you ten.

HH: That's more like it. *Ten?* Are you trying to insult me? Me with a poor dying grandmother? *Ten?*

B: (*Urgently.*) All right, I'll give you eleven.

HH: *Now* you're getting it! *Eleven!* This cost me twelve! You want to ruin me?

B: (*Frantic.*) Seventeen?

HH: No, no, you go to fourteen now.

B: All right, I'll give you fourteen.

HH: Fourteen? Are you joking?

B: Fifteen!

HH: Seventeen. It's my last word. I won't take a penny less, or strike me dead!

B: Sixteen.

HH: Done! Nice to do business with you.

As you can see, a measured, strategic outlook will help in even the most basic price negotiations, where speed and simplicity are primary. (Our friend Harry, above, excels at building a rapid-fire value proposition.) It's even more beneficial in advanced bargaining, where talks move beyond price to an array of other issues, as is typically the case in supply chain or account management. And it's absolutely imperative for any move across the continuum toward a broader, more comprehensive, more valuable deal.

We deploy five negotiating strategies in our planning process:

- **Leverage building.** While people dependably react—or overreact—to the power wielded by the other side, they often underestimate their own. One way to strengthen your position is to look at the deal from the other person's standpoint. *Critical questions*: How much strength do I have coming into this negotiation—could it be more than I thought? I know I'm feeling heat to close the deal, but what pressure is the other party under? How can I create more options for myself—or narrow options for them?

- **Discovery.** To assess your leverage you'll need data—and the more the better. Done well, discovery will reveal the other side's flexibility. *Critical questions:* Who can help me with reconnaissance and inside information? Before we get down to numbers, how can I guesstimate the zone of possible agreement (ZOPA)—"the range of options that should be acceptable to both sides"?[2] How can I learn more about my counterpart's needs and vulnerabilities without confiding too much about my own?

- **Target-setting.** Setting high expectations is a prerequisite for getting a better deal. When you put those expectations forward, you'll need a logical narrative to support them. *Critical questions:* What do I want to get out of this deal? Where should I anchor my opening position, and how can I support it? What's my bottom line—the least I'm willing to accept (as a seller) or the most I'm willing to pay (as a buyer)? Can I afford to walk away from this deal? Do I have a strong best alternative to a negotiated agreement (BATNA)?

- **Concession-making.** Knowing when and how much to concede is a core element of negotiation. *Critical questions*: Should I ever make the first concession? How large should my concessions be? How can I carve out more negotiating space? If the bargaining stalls, should I agree to split the difference?

- **Identifying issues.** Not every deal can be made on price alone. *Critical questions:* What can I gain through more favorable terms and conditions (T's & C's) to make up for concessions on price? What values do I bring to the table *beyond* a competitive price? How can I map those values to define the total cost of ownership, or TCO? Can this deal be expanded to make it better for both sides?

Bargaining is rooted in power. It revolves around who has more of it and how they choose to yield it. While power is clearly at the core of leverage building, it overlays the other strategies as well:

- Discovery links to the power of information

- Target-setting to the power of commitment

- Concession-making to the power of reciprocation

- Identifying issues to the power of creativity

Our strategies aren't rigidly linear. They interact and overlap, and you may find yourself skipping ahead or reversing course as a negotiation unfolds. But neither is the ordering random. One common mistake is to set targets before weighing the power/pressure balance and gleaning as much information as you can. Jumping the gun can lead to wild misestimates of the ZOPA. As a result, a seller may open way too low or, less commonly, unreasonably high.

This ties to a broader point: The lion's share of strategizing takes place *before* you sit down to bargain. *Creative negotiators are strategic planners.* You can't count on inspiration at the bargaining table. Establishing your leverage, formulating your questions, setting targets and fallbacks, honing your concessions all need to be initiated in advance. Admittedly, much of our preparation will be speculative, to be tested in the tactical battle to come. As you learn more, you'll likely adjust or refine your approach. Even so, we can testify that positive outcomes are directly correlated to the quality and quantity of prep work.

Planning entails more than ideal-world analysis. (As they say in the military: "If your plan is working perfectly, it's probably an ambush.") Beyond plotting your position and graphing your angle of attack, you need to ready yourself psychologically for the other side's curveballs and your own internal resistance. For example, you've put in the research and come up with a credible anchor price—it's aggressive but not crazy. But come time to pull the trigger, in the heat of contention, you're thrown off balance and wimp out with a more reasonable number. To avoid conflict, you junk your plan and hope for the best. If the other side is more firmly steeled to see their own plan through, you'll likely finish second.

In bridging from planning to execution, our mental models must be primed for the fray. You might emulate Harry the Haggler. No matter how Brian responds, Harry has his counter down cold. When Brian falters, Harry prompts and prods him to do a better job. While the scene is satirically farfetched, it speaks to something real—it's impossible to bargain without some minimal collaboration, at the least a joint engagement in the process. Helping the other side negotiate becomes even more of a necessity as we move along the continuum, from the back-and-forth of haggling to the give-and-take of advanced bargaining and creative dealmaking. In his insistence on arriving at a mutually satisfying outcome, Harry is thinking like a negotiator, all the way.

1. Leverage Building

Let's turn to another cinema classic, *National Lampoon's Vacation*.[3] Chevy Chase plays Clark Griswold, a Chicago food processing salesman about to drive his family to Walley World, a Los Angeles theme park. The day before their departure, Clark and his teenaged son swing by the local dealer's lot to pick up their sleek new car. It's the Super Sportswagon in Antarctic blue, with an optional Rally Fun Pack. But the salesman tells them the model they'd ordered has been delayed for six weeks. He has another vehicle that's far superior, he insists, for a cross-country drive: the Wagon Queen Family Truckster in metallic pea, a hideous shade of green. ("You think you hate it now, but wait until you drive it!") Distraught, Clark discovers that the trade-in he'd dropped off minutes earlier has already been pancaked in the compacter. Baited and switched, he reluctantly takes home the Truckster and sings its praises to his long-suffering wife.

What happened to Clark is an object lesson in leverage building, the alpha dog of bargaining strategies, the one that overlays all the rest. Discovery is designed to test our power hypotheses. The targets we set are determined by the competitive leverage we can bring to bear. And how much we concede depends on how badly we need the deal.

Time

Time is the universal stressor in any negotiation. As lead times shorten and schedules constrict, the boss wants it cheaper *and* faster. Everybody's on perpetual deadline. If you believe that time is on your side, it probably pays to be patient. String the talks out and put off any quick resolution. Since sellers are almost always under pressure to make their numbers, there's an inverse relationship between the timeline and the price line. The more protracted the negotiation, the more pressure on the seller to lower the price. But what gets overlooked is the pressure on the *buyer*, though it may be less obvious or acute. Clark Griswold had next to no power on the car lot because he'd promised his family a vacation the next morning—and the salesman knew it.

Authority

Clark caved on the Family Truckster in the face of the salesman's superior expertise: *I know more about cars than you do, and this is the right model for you.* But while knowledge gaps are real, they can be narrowed with research. One of our client companies in Europe was proud of its mission of sustainability and generally gave preference to companies that shipped on returnable pallets instead of cheaper disposables. A smart seller did some spadework and led their presentation with hosannas for their fuel-efficient delivery trucks, their cogenerated electrical power, their extensive water treatment practices—*and* their reusable pallets. Though their bid was higher than others, the green seller got the deal. They won out because they'd gone beyond the request for proposal (RFP) to learn what the customer valued.

Authority comes in different flavors. Technical minutiae matter less than a well-prepared strategy. The superior negotiator will usually carry the day, even when bargaining from an objectively weaker position. A mastery of strategies and tactics makes for a winning mindset. There's no more potent source of leverage than that.

Commitment

We can only imagine how many hours a fellow like Clark Griswold spent poring over Kelly's Blue Book and back issues of *Car and Driver* before settling on the car and options he wanted and targeting a dealer with a good price. He'd invested so much effort that it would have pained him to leave the lot without a new car—*any* new car.

When facing a committed seller, some buyers will intentionally drag things out to get the seller even *more* committed and amenable to making concessions. Keep in mind the other side's workload and all the other projects waiting on their plate. The last thing they'll want to do is start *this* job over from scratch. Their work pressure—their time and effort expended—is your leverage.

Risk

The greater your willingness to risk deadlock, or no deal, the more power you'll accrue—and the more leverage to drive a harder bargain. Given Clark's time pressures, he'd be taking a big chance in walking off the lot without a car. Beyond his time crunch, he'd be running a reputational risk. He'd doubtless raved about the new car to his wife and coworkers, not to mention his adolescent son. Coming home empty-handed would have been tough to stomach. (Clark's family was yet another source of leverage for the seller: *organizational pressure.*)

Creating (or Taking Away) Options

Once Clark's old car was crushed, he had no good choices— his goose was cooked. Buyers gather leverage by coming up with more options: alternate suppliers for the same item, an alternate technology (cloud storage vs. physical hard drives), even a lesser-quality item that will suffice for their needs. Sellers create leverage by finding other potential buyers to bid against one another. One client of ours, a power transformer manufacturer, was known for laying down the law to prospective buyers. "The price was the price"—and if they wouldn't pay it, he could make a single phone call and ship his product to China instead. When supply-and-demand is working in their favor, sellers can shrink a buyer's options by showing they may soon be out of stock.

Legitimacy

Knowing Clark, we're guessing that he agreed to pay full sticker price for the Super Sportswagon or at least something close to it. Unlike casual verbal price quotes, professionally printed window stickers or hotel rate cards add leverage to a seller's position. The same goes for well-designed website pricing charts. People are more reluctant to challenge prices at Best Buy than at a mom-and-pop neighborhood shop, though they may be equally negotiable.

Buyers also lean on legitimacy: "Those are our standard T's & C's, everybody complies with them." Or: "This RFP lists our precise specs, and we expect you to meet them to the letter." If the requirements are printed on heavy stock, they carry even more weight.

Persistence

You repeatedly say no to the price but persist in asking questions and keeping the talks afloat until the seller comes down. Conversely, the last seller left standing in the ring may win the deal by default. Persistent negotiators aren't fazed when the other side stops returning their calls—they refuse to be discouraged. As the saying goes, "Never take no answer for a 'no' answer." Your simple willingness to hang in there can be a deceptively potent source of leverage.

2. Discovery

In bargaining, the main point of discovery is to test the other side's limits. Whether by asking for more or telling them *no*, you'll get a read on how much flexibility they have—and whether they're bluffing when they tell you, "That's our bottom line number—it's the best I can do."

The more information you have, the better you'll be able to assess your power relative to the other side's. You'll also acquire more credibility. Creative bargainers argue vigorously for their positions but aren't entrenched in their prejudgments—nobody's right all the time, after all. They're open to the possibility of learning something useful that will modify their stance. Tactical retreats may pave the way for strategic victories. The tone is set with three simple words: *Tell me more.* You're not necessarily agreeing, but you're showing you'll consider their point of view.

Discovery addresses a host of issues:

- Who has more power in this negotiation? Are there flaws in my assumptions? Do I have as much leverage as I thought?

- How motivated is the other side to come to an agreement?

- Are their expectations realistic, or do they need to be brought down to earth?

- Does it look like we have a ZOPA, even if I can't discern exactly what it is? Is it possible we'll be walking away without a deal?

- What are the pressures on the other side, and how can I turn them to my advantage?

- What do I need out of this deal? (Spoiler alert: It may not be what you think you want.) Are *my* expectations out of line?

- Is there something I've overlooked that could make the deal more valuable to my organization or possibly to both?

- What's subjectively important to the other side beyond price?

Some of the most valuable discovery takes place in advance. A diligent negotiator will mine public data or tap colleagues with inside dope on the other organization. Once armed with these insights, you'll be ready for the face-to-face phase of discovery. There's an art to eliciting information in an adversarial setting. It's less about hitting a bull's-eye on the first try and more about gradually zeroing in. To get a handle on personal or organizational pressures, you might lead with small talk before cutting to the chase. In the relationship-building mode, one tried-and-true tactic is *not* to get to the point, at least not too abruptly. Even in bargaining, which moves at a quicker tempo, it can help to be indirect at the start.

Creative negotiators put themselves in the other person's shoes rather than trying to cram the other side into their own. As the playwright Arthur Miller reminds us, "If you don't understand the viewpoint, you don't understand the price."[4] It always helps to bring some open-ended questions. (Try starting with *why* or *how*.) Then listen attentively to the other side's answers, hearing them out without judgment or defensiveness. Say a seller has set their price at $100 per unit, well over the buyer's budget or what they've paid in the past. To angle for a quick concession, the buyer could respond, "We can't pay that," leaving the seller to twist slowly. But another option would be to dig for more information:

- A hundred dollars? From our experience, that seems high. Could you explain how you arrived at that number?

- What can you tell us about your cost factors? (That's proprietary information and they probably won't tell you, but it never hurts to ask.)

- I'm a little confused here. Why has the price gone up?

Once people are engaged in civil conversation, tension is defused. The temperature in the room drops. By acknowledging the cooperative aspect of a competitive process (*We're both here to find a solution*), you'll help the other side relax. Bargaining may be a game of hardball, but all games involve human interaction. Negotiators aren't derivatives traders; deals don't get made with the push of a button. Even when the process seems purely transactional, there are always two or more people working with and against one another. There's a social exchange as well as a financial one.

Sometimes a warmer atmosphere is all that's needed for an unexpected concession. At the least, it can help reveal an unseen source of friction. We were working with one of the world's largest construction companies when they hit a wall with a private firm that made a gigantic, one-of-a-kind pump. The company's founder named an exorbitant price, way out of whack with industry standards. Our client kept upping their offer, but the founder refused to budge: "No, I need this much for my pump."

They went around and around for weeks, until someone was clever enough to ask: "But *why* do you need that much for your pump?"

The founder replied, "Because I'm afraid you'll start making them yourselves." He pictured this powerful *Fortune* 500 company producing their own giant pumps and possibly putting him out of business. He'd padded his price to be set for life should his worst-case fear come to pass. When our client gave him an ironclad guarantee to noncompete, the founder happily shaved his price in half. He wasn't a gouger; he just needed some peace of mind.

Finally, keep in mind that discovery is a two-way street. To get the information you're after, you may have to give some up in turn. What counts is to be deliberate in what you're willing to disclose and protect your leverage. This should be an explicit part of the planning/preparation process—laid down in writing, if possible.

3. Target-Setting

Once you've built your leverage and confirmed it through discovery, you're ready to set your goal for the deal. To be precise, you'll be setting three goals. From higher to lower, they are:

- The *anchor*, an aspirational starting point to give yourself trading room and curb the other side's expectations.

- The *target*, a realistic estimate of what you think you can achieve if the negotiation goes reasonably well.

- The *reservation price* (also known as the *walk-away* or *bottom line*), the most a buyer is willing to pay or the least a seller will accept. When the two overlap, there's a ZOPA, the basis for an agreement.

Let's consider each of these in turn.

The Anchor

In *Thinking, Fast and Slow,* Daniel Kahneman recounts a fascinating experiment with visitors to the San Francisco Exploratorium. One group was asked these two questions:

Is the height of the tallest redwood more or less than 1,200 feet?

What is your best guess about the height of the tallest redwood?

A second group received the same questions, with one difference: the reference point changed from 1,200 feet to 180 feet. When asked for their best guesses, the first group guessed that the tallest redwood was 844 feet. The second group put it at only 282 feet.[5] (In point of fact, the tallest redwood—the tallest tree in the world—stands at 380 feet.)

Psychologists call this mechanism "priming," the use of subtle cues on a person's subconscious automatic system. Suggesting a number, even a random one, has a profound impact on how people interpret what comes next. In *Pre-Suasion,* Robert Cialdini relates a consultant's frustrations in negotiating a fair price for his work. Though he refused on principle to pad his budget, his clients routinely asked for 10 or 15 percent off. As a consequence, he'd either be gutting his profit margin or risk losing the job. Until he accidentally hit upon a solution:

> After his standard presentation and just before declaring his ($75,000) fee, he joked, "As you can tell, I'm not going to be able to charge you a million dollars for this." The client looked up from the written proposal he'd been studying and said, "Well, I can agree to that!" The meeting proceeded without a single subsequent reference to compensation and ended with a signed contract.[6]

When the consultant followed the same script with other clients, it worked like a charm. Though it didn't always lead to a contract, it clinched his fair fee whenever he got one. The moral? *Anchor high as a seller; anchor low as a buyer.* Human beings are susceptible to what Ariely calls "arbitrary coherence." Although an initial price may be arbitrary, "once those prices are established in our minds, they shape not only what we are willing to pay for an item, but also how much we are willing to pay for related products."[7] Your anchor will frame the other side's expectations for both the deal at hand and any follow-up deals in the future.

Our own research confirms this axiom of the trade: *Negotiators who ask for more get more.* Your opening bid imprints an idea that alters how the other side perceives the ZOPA. It's why similar homes in comparable locations sell at widely different numbers, in direct correlation with their asking prices. You can't fully test the other side's flexibility without a strong anchor, one that pushes the limits without seeming unrealistic. Besides, you have little to lose. If you're a buyer and start out by asking for a 15 percent reduction, you can still settle later for 10 percent. But if you open at 10, it's safe to say the seller will balk at backtracking to 15, even if they can afford it. For that matter, it's unlikely you'll get the full 10 percent, since people assume there's at least a little give in your opening position.

Anchoring is valuable for defense as well as offense. At the left of the continuum, in particular, there are many unknowns. When we jump into bargaining with someone new, we can't be sure about who we're dealing with, the quality of what they're offering, or how reliable they'll be if something goes wrong down the road. As a negotiation proceeds, and the other side proves transparent and trustworthy, we'll naturally be freer in exchanging information and more open to compromise. But even in the best case, life strays from our best-laid plans. Market conditions fluctuate over the term of a contract. Factories shut down; trusted contacts move to other jobs. Recessions and pandemics may rear their ugly heads. *To protect ourselves, it's imperative to leave room for contingencies.* A solid anchor does just that.

The Target

Your anchor plays off your target, a positive outcome that seems reasonably attainable—which means the target needs to be set first. In a perfect world, targets would be governed by objective analysis. What we've found, however, is that they waft in the winds of subjectivity and suggestibility. In one seminar exercise, a top-of-the-line, wood-fired pizza oven had an asking price of $95,000.

All buyers and sellers received the same background data—with one exception. We told one group that the average negotiation at previous seminars had settled at $90,000, and a second group that the mean negotiated price was $80,000. After they'd completed the activity, we polled their results. The first group settled at an average of $89,000, and the second group at $81,000—same oven, same circumstances, same data. They'd been primed into shading their targets toward the norm.

Both targets and anchors rely on *subjective value*. Agreements get made when I place a higher value on what you're offering than on what I need to give up to get it. As we'll outline in greater detail in the section on creative dealmaking, our targets carry more weight when we build their subjective value with illustration, explanation, and—most of all—a good story. Many buyers will gladly pay above the so-called market price for features of special value to them. Ditto for vendors, who may sell their wares under the going rate if they perceive added value in doing business with an established brand. Often these subjective values are subtle or hidden. It's your job to surface them.

It's easy to set ambitious targets in the planning phase. It gets tougher when you're up against a living, breathing person with a conflicting goal. Targets are only as good as your commitment to defend them. Say you're a seller and know you can trim 10 percent off your target price and still come out okay. If you run into a hard-bargaining buyer, you may find yourself sacrificing that 10 percent very quickly. But suppose you tell your boss beforehand, "At most, I'm going to go down 5 percent." The research shows that sharing your targets with colleagues makes for stronger outcomes.

The Reservation Price

The reservation price is the point where you become indifferent to getting the deal or not—where a "no" looks as good as a "yes." It's the floor or ceiling you will not go beyond: "If I can't get my must-haves, I'm prepared to lose this deal."

While it's vital for negotiators to impose limits on concessions, there's also an argument to be made *not* to focus on a precise walk-away point. The reason? As one manager complained to us, "My people won't set a high target and won't stick to what they set. They're so desperate to get the deal that the second the buyer says, 'You're out of the ballpark,' they go straight to their bottom line." Many negotiators fail to realize that they can stand staunchly behind their targets without losing the deal. In a high-pressure environment, a reservation price can become a self-fulfilling prophecy, a safe harbor to relieve the tension of conflict.

Whether or not you set a reservation price, it's mandatory to formulate a palatable plan B—your BATNA. As William Ury notes, a Plan B guarantees that your interests "are respected *even if* the other side does not cooperate."[8] Maybe it means finding a new customer or drumming up resources inhouse. Looked at dispassionately, in the cold light of day, the worst-case scenario is often not so bad.

Without a BATNA, you're on your heels from the start: *I can't afford to lose this deal.* With a credible BATNA, you can set a more aggressive target. That's another argument for strenuous prenegotiation planning. In general, the more deeply you reflect upon your target, the better you'll understand why you want to make the deal. You'll be better able to adopt the mindset you need to get the deal done—on terms that make sense for you.

4. Concession-Making

In *Planes, Trains and Automobiles*, Neal Page, a marketing executive played by Steve Martin, negotiates for a taxi in midtown Manhattan.

> Neal Page: Sir? Sir, sir, excuse me, I know this is your cab, but I'm desperately late for a plane and was wondering if I could appeal to your good nature and ask you to let me have it.
>
> Other Man: (*Sliding into the cab.*) I don't have a good nature; excuse me.
>
> NP: Can I offer you ten dollars for it?

OM: Hah!

NP: Twenty, I'll give you twenty dollars for it.

OM: I'll take fifty. (*Sees SM digging into his pocket.*) Anyone who'd pay fifty dollars for a cab would certainly pay seventy-five.

NP: Not necessarily—all right, seventy-five. You're a thief!

OM: Close. I'm an attorney.[9]

Concessions contain a paradox. They're often the express route for getting the deal, or at least getting closer to it. The catch is that they may also have the opposite effect, moving you *further* from an agreement. How is that possible? Miscalculated concessions suggest that you've padded your anchor and lack confidence in your values. Since bargaining is at its heart a *taking* mode, excessive and unreciprocated giving raises the other side's expectations. It whets their appetite for *more* concessions, perhaps more than you're able or willing to make. Give up too much too soon, and soon you're staring at your bottom line—with no room to move. Your weight is so far on your back foot that you're toppling over.

For creative negotiators, the challenge is to concede in a way that gets you from your opening position to a close without blowing past your target. Again, it helps to remind yourself that *both* sides are under pressure. When we keep that in mind, it opens our eyes and stiffens our spines.

Slow, Small, and Considered

An effective concession strategy shores up your anchor and target by putting the onus to concede on the other side:

> **After you!** In most cases, the party who makes the initial concession ends up with a below-average settlement. How do you coax the other side to go first? The watchword is *patience*. Slow the process down, and let the tension curve rise. If they're slow to volunteer, begin with a question: "We're pretty far apart. Do you have any room to move?"

When all else fails, and you're stuck on square one, tender a concession that leaves your pricing intact and doesn't raise the other side's expectations. Rather than abandoning your anchor prematurely, you might say, "This is the price I need, but here's what I can do for you. Our policy is to pay our bills within sixty days, but tell you what—I'll call in a favor from accounting and pay you in thirty. And you can do the installation around your schedule instead of ours." The buyer is sending a confident message: My budget is reasonable. By the same token, sellers can use minor concessions to assert that their price is fair, not inflated. By invoking the powerful social norm of reciprocation, you may induce the other side to make a *major* concession on price in return.

> **Be stingy.** Large concessions smack of desperation. Better to keep them smaller and leave some room beyond your target— say, 10 percent. You won't know how badly the other person wants the deal, so here's a way to find out. Instead of conceding the 10 percent in one gulp, offer 2 percent. If that doesn't get the deal done, try another 2 percent, and so on. If they bite before you reach your target, more power (and profit) to you. The downside: you could wind up giving the entire 10 percent and leave the other side thinking, "There has to be another 2 percent in there." To steer clear of this trap, you might . . .
>
> **Slow down.** With the same 10 percent to play with, you might make a slightly larger first concession, maybe 3 percent. If that doesn't get the deal, your next move down is 2 percent, then 1.5 percent, then 1 percent, then half a percent. What message are you sending? *You're nearing the end of the line.* The result? The other side's hopes are gently deflated. By digging in just a little harder, you may wind up saving 2 percent. On a $10 million deal, that's $200,000 in profit.
>
> **Stay calm at the deadline.** In our experiments, we've found that most people stay reasonably disciplined through most of the process—only to lose their equilibrium toward the end out of fear of losing the deal. While you may need

to prepare to concede as a deadline closes in, do so incrementally. A massive eleventh-hour concession will only dig a deeper hole, as it did for Steve Martin's character. When you're about to say *yes*, say *no* one more time: "That 7 percent price drop isn't going to work." Then see what they do next. Meanwhile, you're giving your reflective system a chance to kick in.

Don't split the difference . . . unless it's to your advantage. You're relatively close to an agreement and the other side proposes meeting halfway. Given the chance to end the discomfort of conflict, you find it tempting to agree. But it's a mistake to say *yes* before probing for more flexibility. If the two parties are $10 per unit apart, why not concede $2.50 instead of $5? There's nothing inherently fair about splitting down the middle. If you persist in asking for more, you might be able to leverage the other side's weariness into a better deal.

Exceptions: After a protracted haggle, you're ready to take the other side's offer . . . or you've already exceeded your target and would be delighted to settle there. Instead, offer to meet in the middle. You might get that little bit extra while seeming to be flexible and even generous, which could work to your favor in the future.

Build in some straw issues. There's an old Jewish fable about a poor man who lived with his wife and six children in a small one-room home. There was so little space they could barely breathe. Tempers were frayed; life couldn't be worse. Dismayed, the man went to his rabbi, who told him, "Bring in all of your animals to share your house." Though the man was perplexed, he herded in his cow and two goats and six chickens. The house became a nightmare of noise and smells and chaos. Life was unbearable! The man ran back to his rabbi for more advice. This time he was told to move the animals back outside. The next day, the man went to the rabbi with a big smile on his face, "Our life is so good now! The animals are out of the house and we have space to spare. What a joy!"[10]

One way to build in trading room is to include a few items you know you could concede without pain—an extended payment schedule, for example. Besides helping to defend the integrity of your anchor, these "goats and chickens" will make the other side appreciative when you give them up.

> **Push for a quid pro quo.** After bargaining for days, it looks like the other side isn't coming off their last number, which is well within your ZOPA. Rather than conceding unilaterally, probe to see how they might offer something in return. Ask for a timeout if you need one, "Give me a minute to think this over." Or, "Let me check with the office and get right back to you." Take a pause and consider how they could sweeten the pot beyond price . . . which brings us to our final bargaining strategy.

5. Identifying Issues

A few years ago, a fellow we knew as the Admiral gave us a window on how bargaining has changed over the last twenty-five years. Back in the 1990s, when he became director of one of the nation's largest purchasing organizations, budgets were flush and pricing was deemphasized. To get top quality, most of his procurement people were paying list price or near it.

But as the industry came under pressure from offshore competition, he explained, "I was getting heat from my executive team to find ways to take out more cost. So I gave my people formal negotiating training, and they learned new tactics to pressure their suppliers. When we purchased big-ticket items like diesel generators, my top people would be getting 15 percent discounts. Most of the rest were in the 10 to 12 percent range.

"I felt pretty satisfied. But then I noticed something. As the business changed from basic products to packages of services and solutions, my top folks were still bringing back those whopper

15 percent reductions. My immediate reaction was, 'Congratulations, that's a great job negotiating!' But then I took a closer look and said, 'Wait a minute, a customer our size should be getting guaranteed lead times and extended payment terms. I don't see those in here.'

"And they said, 'No, we couldn't get them at this price.'

"'What about first install support? And training?' Dead silence. And I said, 'Wow, I hope we're not getting just their standard warranty—that could put us up the creek without a paddle.'

"And they said, 'No, we're not getting the standard warranty.'

"'Well, that's a relief!'

"'Actually, to get this price, our team had to cancel the warranty altogether.'"

That's when the Admiral spoke the immortal words: "You got a great price, all right, but you made a lousy deal!"

We heard similar complaints from other sourcing directors and sales directors. Likewise from the people directing project managers, who'd get laser-focused on the cost of a change order to the exclusion of all else. Bargaining had changed ahead of the bargainers. It was more intricate and complex, but the people doing the negotiating were stuck in the haggling mud. They were trapped by their old mental models. To advance from a *good price* to a *good deal*, they needed a different approach. That insight inspired the Mobus Negotiating Continuum.

To this day, there are times when buyers need a quick agreement and aren't interested in the subtleties: *Just give me your best price.* Though they may not get the optimal outcome, they'll accept the tradeoff to save time. In other instances, deals get so complex that front-line bargainers throw up their hands and say, "I don't even know where to start—the *only* thing I can grab on to is price." Often they're still being assessed and rewarded by one-dimensional, price-heavy metrics. What organizations practice may diverge from what they preach.

Even so, it can't be ignored that most deals today involve more moving parts than they did twenty years ago. Getting that healthy discount is no longer enough. Today's question is: What are we leaving *out* of this deal? It's now compulsory to look at issues beyond price. Through rigorous prenegotiation planning and active discovery, buyers will get a handle on all of the elements that comprise the familiar acronym, *TCO*: total cost of ownership. It's the difference between a $60,000 BMW and a comparable $66,000 Lexus—which is more expensive? When you figure in the Lexus's superior mileage and the BMW's higher service costs, the answer isn't so obvious.

Modern buyers are on the hunt for additional net value and are willing to pay more upfront to get it. They're also keen to hear from the seller about items in the RFP that might be modified or even dispensed with to reduce their TCO. When two parties feel stranded far apart on price, this value-based approach can bridge the gap.

In today's buy/sell environment, top negotiators may hold off on signing even when their price demands are met and all their boxes checked. Advanced bargaining is still a zero-sum game of exploiting the other side's weaknesses. But as we make tradeoffs on price to reap added value, we're playing chess now, not checkers. A buyer's top-of-mind goal is not to save money, per se, but to lower the TCO. Even when sellers seem inflexible on price, they may be surprisingly open to discuss other deal points.

The trick is to find the not-so-obvious issues that can make the difference. Once again, this requires advance planning. First, think through *past* issues:

- How did I get here?

- Why am I thinking about switching to this new item or service?

- What are the transition costs in switching?

- How can I minimize those costs through the negotiation?

Then turn to *future* issues, all the things buyers wish they'd thought of after the fact:

- **Training:** How do our people use this wonderful thing we've bought?

- **Warranties/service contract:** What can go wrong, and how will it be fixed?

- **Future needs:** What might we need in a year or even ten years from now? (We should ask for it now.)

- **Upgrades:** What's likely to change down the road? Can we get an option on the next-gen product?

- **Price protection:** How long is the agreed-upon price good for?

In some cases, a sweetener can do more to boost a buyer's profits than a substantial price cut. A seller, meanwhile, might be happy to lower the price in exchange for relief on specs or a modified warranty. Instead of making a Hobson's choice between shredding their margin or blowing the deal, creative negotiators tackle third-way questions: *Why are they asking for a discount? And why 5 percent? Is that what they really need? Could something else work better for them?*

Advanced bargaining marks the first mile of a negotiator's journey from winning to problem-solving. It's not such a long stretch from finding one-way TCO concessions to *trading* concessions and expanding the joint *TBO,* or total business opportunities. That's where we begin to move from distributing value to enlarging the pie, to a bilateral matching of assets and needs—to creative dealmaking.

Summary

- A strategic outlook will yield superior results even in basic price bargaining.

- In the bargaining mode, the prime strategy is *leverage building.* Creative bargainers leverage time, authority, legitimacy, their willingness to risk deadlock, and the other side's commitment to the deal. And they persist in the face of resistance.

- *Discovery* tests the other side's limits and flexibility. You're out to determine which side comes into the negotiation with more power. But whatever the power balance, a friendly conversation can reveal the other party's needs and even lead to unexpected concessions.

- *Target-setting* is a three-part exercise: your *anchor*, your aspirational starting point; your *target*, a reasonable estimate for where you think you'll land; and your *reservation price*, the point where you'd be willing to walk away from the deal.

- *Concessions* are double-edged. They can move you closer to a deal or further away from one. Creative negotiators concede slowly, calmly, and in small increments. They agree to split the difference only when it works in their favor.

- A good price doesn't necessarily equate to a good deal. By *identifying issues* beyond price and exploring what the other side really needs, creative bargainers can increase their net profits.

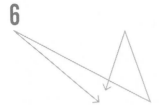

6

Bargaining Tactics

Where strategies point us in the direction of our goal, tactics are the power levers for getting there. By accentuating pressure on the other side, they lower expectations, shape motivations, and drive people toward their bottom line. The creative negotiator's challenge is twofold: to wield these tactics adeptly, and to keep antennae up for the other side's tactical moves. Succeed on both fronts, and odds are good that you'll win the competitive leverage game.

To some, haggling tactics may connote less-than-scrupulous manipulation. But to repeat: bargaining is an adversarial activity. Our job is to gain an advantage and defend our interests. While we wouldn't ordinarily use these techniques on friends or neighbors, negotiating is governed by different rules. It's like pulling up a chair to a poker game. The other players figure that you'll bluff from time to time, and no one would expect you to show your cards in the middle of a hand. You play the way the game is played. As Don Lucchesi said in *The Godfather, Part III*, "It's not personal, it's business."

And so the question becomes: Where do we draw the boundary between gamesmanship and deception? Between withholding pieces of information and out-and-out deception? While some tactics tread closer to the line than others, context matters. Your prior history and level of trust with the other party factor into the calculus, as do the ploys being used against you. But here's a rule of thumb: If a tactic might undermine your future credibility, it's probably a bad idea. Deliberate disinformation isn't kosher. It's one thing for a buyer to tell the lowest bidder that the price is more than they want to pay. It's another to flat-out lie and tell them that two other bidders have come in lower. If that's the buyer's M.O., word gets around. Their reputation suffers. Soon their bidders will be coming in higher than they otherwise would have for extra negotiating room.

Creative conflict rests on the understanding that today's adversary could be tomorrow's partner. Integrity isn't just a high-minded notion. It's your passport to more collaborative and more lucrative deals. But how can you protect yourself if the other side proves to be dishonest? Assuming it still makes sense to deal with them at all, you'll need to do more intensive discovery and to get the smallest details in writing. You'll pad your price, as a tax on their unreliability and to cover the overhead for a slower, heavily monitored process. Then, after you've signed, you'll be prepared for more work in executing the deal and following up.

For ease of reference, we've organized our bargaining tactics under their related strategies.

Leverage Tactics

As we've noted, bargaining is a game of leverage—of identifying your advantage and pressing it. Here are some of the most effective ways to do just that.

Take It or Leave It (TIOLI)

HARRY THE HAGGLER. *Seventeen. It's my last word. I won't take a penny less, or strike me dead.*

TIOLI, the classic ultimatum, leaves no apparent choice but to submit or lose the deal. Though it can be invoked at any point, it's used more often toward the end of a negotiation, when one side wishes to convey that they've gone as far as they can. (If used at the beginning, it's more ultimatum than tactic.) TIOLI can be tempered by applying it to limited parts of the deal. For example, you might draw a line in the sand on price but leave some flexibility on terms and conditions.

In business, TIOLI is rarely expressed in so many words. Most people find less inflammatory ways to get the message across. As a salesperson once told us, "That's my doorknob price," meaning he'd turn the knob and walk if we didn't meet it. Other variations on the theme:

- That's the best I can do.

- It's our standard rate.

- It's our company policy.

- It's printed right here in black and white.

- That's as far as I'm authorized to go.

TIOLI plays off *legitimacy*—the power of authority—to support an aggressive opening bid. Then the other side has to ask themselves: Is this real, or is it a leverage-building ploy? If accepted at face value, TIOLI becomes self-fulfilling. If you're on the receiving end, you might try to chip away at it: "What if we could pay cash in ten days? Could you do a little better then?" If you push back hard enough, or simply ignore it, TIOLI may be exposed for the posturing it often is.

> Harry the Haggler: Seventeen. It's my last word. I won't take a penny less, or strike me dead!
>
> Brian: Sixteen.
>
> Harry: Done! Nice to do business with you.[1]

At times you may need to resort to TIOLI to keep your leverage from seeping away. There's a story involving the late Jack Welch, who was running General Electric, and Phil Condit, the Boeing CEO. Welch did much of his business at lunch, and one day he buttonholed Condit about GE's bid to supply the engines for the new Boeing 777. He wouldn't stop pestering the guy. Finally, Condit told him that GE basically had the deal, but that Welch couldn't tell his people. Over the next three months, Boeing squeezed GE's negotiators for one price concession after the next. Welch couldn't stand it any longer. He told Condit he'd have to break his commitment to keep quiet—at which point Condit advised him to tell his troops to go back with a firm TIOLI. The deal closed that day.[2]

An effective TIOLI requires a strong power position. It implies that you can live without the deal and are willing to run the risk of losing it. When items are commoditized and the market contains numerous similar options, the tactic works better for buyers than for sellers. (If Brian hadn't been in such a hurry, he could have turned the tables on Harry the Haggler in a New York minute.) One more point: if you do use TIOLI, be prepared for the tension and resentment that hardball haggling can provoke.

Higher Authority

When confronted with an implacable TIOLI, one time-honored counter is to ask your boss to call the other side's boss and ask to get a fair shot at the deal. As you move up the ladder, final offers become more flexible.

Best and Final Offer (BAFO)

Here's another maneuver that makes the person on the receiving end wonder if there's any room left to negotiate. Where TIOLI can be employed by either side, BAFO is strictly a buyer's tactic. It's expressed along the lines of, "I don't want to waste my time or yours. Whoever comes in lowest will get the business, so give me your best shot up front."

While a BAFO is rarely accepted as truly final, it can narrow the price gap—and thereby clarify the ZOPA—before talks begin. By pressing sellers to squeeze any fat out of their proposal, this tactic puts buyers in the driver's seat. Even when the seller complies, there's nothing to stop the buyer from bargaining down to the seller's next best price. The downside: once a BAFO is deployed, the cooperative side of creative conflict flies out the door. When sellers feel squeezed out of the gate, they're unlikely to volunteer how a job might be better structured or to clue the buyer in on something missing from the specs. They'll cut corners to deliver a rock-bottom price, knowing they can take their revenge with change orders later on.

Should a seller knuckle under to a BAFO, not knowing if it's real? The answer may hinge on your circumstances. If business is booming, it's easier to be a price hawk and anchor high. If sales are really slow, and you've lost the last three projects you bid on, it's more difficult to roll the dice. But though it's a calculated risk, sellers are usually better served by *not* coming in with their very best offer. One way to escape the BAFO straitjacket is to submit a reasonably low bid while injecting points of ambiguity. Then you can say, "Our proposal has a lot of subtleties. Let's set aside an hour and I'll walk you through it." If the buyer agrees, you'll have another opportunity to justify your price. You might even get some ideas on how to lower it without hurting your profit, like paving with macadam instead of concrete.

Tactical Deadline

Time pressure forces action. As quarter's end approaches, sales-people ramp up their efforts to close more deals and are more open to shaving their margins. But when orders back up and end users are clamoring for quick delivery, buyers come to the bargaining table with one hand tied behind their backs.

Time constraints are baked into the negotiating process. Savvy negotiators will intensify them to pressure the other side. Buyers may layer a tactical deadline atop a BAFO: "You've got till three o'clock Friday to give us your best bid or we'll have to start talking to somebody else." Or a salesperson will warn: "I can only hold this price until the end of the week, then a surcharge kicks in."

Tactical deadlines are more persuasive when their targets are up against organizational deadlines as well. If you know the other side is under internal pressure, you can turn the screw even tighter. Conversely, if your organization has handed you a deadline, you might try to extend it to expand your negotiating room.

Tactical Deadlock

This is the neutron bomb of tactics. Let's say you've made your presentation and run into stiff resistance. You have more to say, maybe more ground to give; you expect the stalemate to pass and the bargaining to resume. But to soften up the other side, you choose to leave the negotiations knowing full well you have other options. (This is a horse of a different color from walking out when you've hit a genuine impasse and purposely pull the plug. Not that there's nothing wrong with that. If it's a bad deal, you're gaining value in reverse by killing it.)

The tactical deadlock is a high-risk, high-reward gambit. Nothing rattles a person's confidence so much as seeing a deal they were counting on suddenly vanish out the door. There's no better way to test their resolve, heighten their anxiety, or lower their aspirations. There's no more powerful message you can send.

On the surface, a deadlock sounds like the easiest thing in the world to execute. "I'm sorry, but it looks like we'll have to go elsewhere," you say, and you pick up your marbles and move to go home—until they come rushing after you with concessions in hand.[3] But for most of us non-econs, a tactical deadlock is emotionally trying to pull off. It creates acute tension, if not outright animosity. It conflicts with our dearest social norm, to get along and be agreeable.

What's more, the chance of losing the deal is real. Sure, you can be polite and hint at future possibilities: "We'd love to work with you, but we just can't do it at that price. Let us know if things change or some additional revenue opens up." But sometimes the other side will let you walk, nevertheless. Maybe they see no recourse, or maybe they're calling your bluff. The jeopardy is magnified when you're bargaining with a regular customer or preferred supplier, or when you harbor hopes for a more creative outcome. Used imprudently, this break-glass move can torpedo a deal and even wreck a relationship. Before trying it, think through the strategic implications. Do the short-term gains outweigh the risks?

The counterargument for the tactic is that you'll be less likely to overpay or undercharge. A car salesman confided to us that customers never get near the dealer's bottom line until they show a willingness to exit the showroom. (Poor Clark Griswold!) If you succeed in closing every single deal you negotiate, perhaps you're not aiming as high as you should.

To mitigate the risk of blowback, we advise people to consult their boss beforehand, and to proceed in partnership with their organization. A tactical deadlock should be considered merely one point on a negotiation's continuum, a moment in time, not the end of the road. Even when the other side lets you go, there are paths back to the table—in reality, you're neither locked nor dead. You may have lost a bit of leverage, but you still have cards to play. Here are three ways to save face and get the talks back on track:

- **You return with new information:** You call them and say, "Something's come up I think you ought to know about." It can be anything under the sun. The point is to get past any awkwardness and revive the dialog.

- **You bring in a relief pitcher:** "Look, I took this as far as I could go. Maybe my boss should talk to your boss."

- **You devise a superior solution:** "I think I've found a way to make this deal better for both of us. Are you interested in hearing what I have to say?" We've used this literally dozens of times and have yet to hear, "No, I don't want to hear your better deal." Just make sure you have the goods to back your claim up.

Discovery Tactics

As you learn more about your adversary's needs, wants, and vulnerabilities, you'll be better able to gauge their flexibility in the negotiation. Some tried and true techniques are given below.

A Walk in the Woods

The tactic's name commemorates an event at the height of the Cold War, when Paul Nitze and his Soviet counterpart took a break from their negotiations on nuclear arms reduction:

> Facing a desperate impasse in their talks, the two men together left the retreat center outside Geneva, Switzerland where they were meeting for, literally, a walk in the woods. The scenic stroll resulted in an unauthorized compromise. . . . During the walk, they discussed shared and divergent concerns, interests, and objectives. They achieved a genuine understanding for what their two countries faced in the escalating arms race. . . .
>
> While their agreement was subsequently rejected by both Moscow and Washington, the saga of their meeting [came] to symbolize the advantages of informal interpersonal bargaining.[4]

In probing for information, *where* and *when* you raise your questions can make all the difference. In formal talks in a business setting, people tend to be tightlipped. You'll have better luck getting them to go off the record on the golf course or at a cocktail party. (For people who are distanced or overscheduled, a simple phone call can also do the trick.) A buyer might start by asking the salesperson some generic questions about their boss, or how business is going, or how the company conducts its sales forecast. Ten or twelve holes (or one or two drinks) in, the buyer arrives at the question that matters: "So do you work on a commission basis?" The seller just might tell you. He might even let slip that he needs to close the deal to make his bonus. In a relaxed environment, social norms come to the fore. Loose lips do indeed sink ships. (Just make sure they're not yours!)

A walk in the woods works wonders with internal business clients, as well. When your engineers or operations people are holding their information infuriatingly close to the vest, take them out to lunch or, better yet, to a ballgame. By the fourth inning or so, you'll be getting an earful.

Leverage the Organization

A casual chat between the two sides' engineers or accountants—or even executive assistants—may divulge more than your front line counterpart. For maximum value, it helps to coach your colleagues before sending them out for intelligence. Negotiators on the procurement side might consider the following:

- How important are we as a customer? Do we represent a wedge into a vertical they're trying to crack?

- Are they hoping to leverage a sale to us to recruit other customers?

- How are their salespeople measured? Do they work on commission or straight salary?

- How badly do they need us right now? Do they have plants running at half capacity? Are they at a point where new business looks good at almost any price?

- Which of their managers or executives are most committed to making the sale?

On the sales side, you might want to find out:

- Who are the buyer's current suppliers? How strong are their relationships?

- Do they have long-term supply agreements in place? If so, when do the contracts expire?

- Have any suppliers recently fallen off in performance, as rated by vendor scorecards?

- What options does the buyer have? Is there something obstructing them from pursuing those options?

- Is the buyer in a bind for product?

- Do they value other issues beyond price and T's & C's? Sustainability? Community development?

- Which of their managers or executives are most committed to making the purchase?

Flinching

BRIAN. I'll give you ten.

HARRY THE HAGGLER. Ten? Are you trying to insult me? Me with a poor dying grandmother? Ten?

Here's an everyday scenario: A seller names a price that seems fair. A weak buyer might say, "That sounds fine, that's in my budget." Or, "Really, is that all?"

A stronger negotiator might say, "That's more than we planned to spend."

A creative bargainer might visibly wince and exclaim, "Wow, that much?" Or a seller might say, "Gee, I'd get fired if I took an offer like that back to my team."

An effective flinch calls on some rudimentary acting skills. The buyer pretends to be shocked and astonished at the proposed price, even if it's half what they expected. They may go on to explain why the price won't work, even when it's entirely acceptable. In any case, they're sending a signal that the seller is in for a rough ride. It's a discovery tactic because it disconcerts the other side into unscripted disclosures. It makes them strain to justify their position.

Flinching might seem a little obvious, but it's more effective than you'd think. Sometimes it works by accident. Mick Ralphs, the British guitar hero for Mott the Hoople and Bad Company, tells a story of how he found his legendary instrument. Since top-of-the-line guitars could be exorbitant, musicians would hunt for bargains in pawn shops. One day, during Mott's first US tour, Ralphs came across a rare 1958 Gibson Les Paul Jr., a vintage model valued up to $25,000 in excellent condition. As Ralphs told the story, he feigned ignorance and asked the pawnbroker, "How much is that guitar in the window, the red one?"

And the pawnbroker said, "You mean the Gibson Les Paul?" Ralphs' heart sank. But then the man said, "One hundred dollars."

Scarcely believing his good luck, Ralphs exclaimed, "A hundred dollars?"

And the pawnbroker said, "Well all right, fifty."[5]

Shut Up!

Experienced buyers are comfortable with long stretches of silence, especially when they know they have more leverage. They allow insecure sellers to talk to fill the dead air and just maybe speak out of turn. A buyer could be leafing slowly through a proposal that looks perfectly fair, until the seller leans over and says, "Don't worry about that price, we can do better than that. We're totally flexible." He's made a concession before the buyer could say a word!

"Shut up!" is the antidiscovery tactic, the virtue of staying tight-lipped while coaxing the other side to be less discreet. Frank told the story of a negotiation with an asphalt salesman. They were 50 cents a ton apart, a substantial sum. Finally, the salesman said, "Look, I just can't give you that 50 cents."

Frank said, "If you can't give it to me, who can?"

The guy said, "If anyone can do it, it's my boss."

"Oh, yeah? Do you think he'd give it to me?"

"Sure, why not?"

Needless to say, Frank got the 50 cent discount. Sellers are notorious leakers. They're under unrelenting pressure to get the deal and keep the customer happy, no matter what. If that involves spilling a little confidential information, that's just the price of doing business, right? A few more examples:

- We can get it to you quickly, we've got a surplus of product right now.

- Our stock price is down, we really need to book the revenue.

- I'm up against my quota, I really need the business.

And from the purchasing side:

- Your product is the only one that passed our acceptance test.

- Our engineering people fell in love with your design.

- How soon could you deliver? We're about to have to shut down the line.

- We've got to get this deal wrapped up to launch our campaign by the first of the year.

- The last time we had a change like this, it cost us a fortune.

- By the way, is your price negotiable? (To which there can be only one answer: *Not any more, it isn't.*)

These indiscreet people are not trying to sabotage their own company. They're just not thinking like negotiators. They're following social norms, which condition us to be open, honest, and forthcoming. Unfortunately for them, bargaining runs by market norms, no matter how friendly the conversation might seem. The less I know about your company's inner workings, the better off you are.

Target-Setting Tactics

One of the most powerful ways to fortify your target is by undercutting the other side's.

Lowballing

In some negotiating cultures, it's commonplace to offer one-fourth the asking price, knowing that merchants or vendors start out at least double what they'll accept. Most Americans hesitate to use this tactic out of fear of giving offense. In some situations— and especially when there are longstanding ties between the two parties—their reluctance is well-taken. But whenever there's market uncertainty and a broad spread of possible prices, a lowball

TACTICS AND SUBJECTIVITY

Most businesspeople know how to deal with objective risk. We can assess it quantitatively or draw on a third party's expertise. While knowing the true risk doesn't eliminate it, at least it leads to evidence-based positions.

Subjective risk is a horse of a different color. Some people feel invulnerable, like nothing bad can happen to them. They're the ones who nonchalantly slide into negotiations and make regrettable deals on the phone. But far more common—and no less damaging—is the opposite syndrome, where people inflate a manageable problem into looming calamity. When negotiators exaggerate risk, they're more susceptible to tactics from the other side.

Tactic	Subjective Reaction
Lowballing	Inadequacy
	I don't really understand the market.
Flinching	Embarrassment
	I've gone too far. They think I'm greedy.
Price Squeeze	Insecurity
	Someone's undercutting me. I better come down.
Trash-Talking	Fear of rejection
	I'm in a worse position than I thought.
Nibbling/Escalation	Disappointment; desperation
	I can't afford to blow this deal now.
Tactical Deadline	Panic
	I better just give them what they want.
Tactical Deadlock	Anxiety
	I'm going to lose this deal.

How do you surmount these subjective roadblocks and rebuild your objective leverage? The best defense is to remind yourself that you have more power than you might think. And that the other side has their own pressures and vulnerabilities, as we'll see in the next chapter.

offer can be a potent and rational play. It firmly plants your anchor while challenging the other side's. You'll find out pretty quickly how much flexibility they have. And regardless of what happens next, you've guaranteed yourself plenty of room to negotiate.

Trash-Talking

The best-laid plans to aim high can come undone in a tough bargaining session. Once you move from internal planning to external negotiating, you're no longer pushing an open door. The other side will be out to lower your expectations by any means available, including negative remarks about you, your company, and your offering. It might be something trivial: "The last time we placed an order with you, it came in two days late." Or: "You're a difficult customer, you want everything perfect at the lowest price." In its uglier iterations, trash talk can take the form of a threat: "Believe me, your product is nothing special. If you don't want to do this for me, we'll take our business elsewhere." Or in a postcontractual dispute: "If you can't comply and live up to your commitment, we'll be turning this over to legal."

Trash talk might contain a few nuggets of truth, or it can be fabricated from whole cloth. It doesn't really matter. The point is to throw you off balance and put you on the defensive. No matter how transparently self-serving the other person's comments, our automatic system—our amygdalae-driven pessimism—kicks in. We get that sinking feeling that our target price is dead in the water.

But remember what you learned on the playground: Sticks and stones can't hurt you. Trash talk doesn't alter the objective power balance. It doesn't relieve the pressures on the other side. Let the verbiage roll off your back and stick to your narrative. Even if what they're saying is true, they're not telling the whole story. Your company may have slipped up on occasion, but what about all those other times you went the extra mile? Counter their critique with data—for example, how your on-time performance beats other suppliers. Throw in some third-party testimonials, ideally from people within their own organization. Finally, don't forget that tactics are *tactical*, and usually more bark than bite.

The person talking trash is often taking it less seriously than the one getting dumped on.

Concession Tactics

Concessions are an essential lubricant for most negotiations, but they should always be made with a purpose. The critical questions are *when* and *how much.*

Price Squeeze

Nothing weakens a seller's resolve more quickly than hearing that the competition is at the door with a comparable solution, only cheaper. The price squeeze is designed to convince you to close the purported gap with your unnamed rival, or *else.* Some buyers will couch this tactic in a velvet glove: "We love your company and would really like to do business with you. And I appreciate all the work you put into this proposal, *but . . .*" If you hear one of the following, it's safe to assume you're being squeezed for a concession:

- You'd better sharpen your pencil.

- You've got to do better than that.

- We're ready to sign, but you've got to get in the ballpark.

The deal is left hanging there, within your grasp, if only you'll come off your price. Now you, the seller, are in a spot. Assuming you've anchored reasonably high, you *know* you can do better. And you know the buyer suspects that, too. But if you get rattled and concede too quickly, they'll smell blood in the water and come back for more. ("You're getting closer, *but . . .*)

How can you maintain forward momentum against a price squeeze?

- **Stay committed to your position as you broaden the conversation.** Hold out for your price and emphasize other values—

on-time performance, after-sales service—that you're bringing to the party.

- **Get them to concede something in return.** If you lower your price, exact a quid pro quo on another issue. Refuse to make further moves until they reciprocate.

- **Though the buyer usually has more options, high-end sellers may have a power/pressure advantage in a given deal.** If you believe that's the case, stick to your guns. (This assumes you've done the requisite planning and research.) The buyer might be squeezing *because they know you're their best option.* They may be leading out of weakness to preempt a power move on your part.

- If you have enough leverage, you might make a token concession and then squeeze back with a TIOLI: "That's the best I can do."

As you'll see, the price squeeze plays a starring role in our dramatic case study in the next chapter.

The Nibble

"Okay, it looks like we've settled all the big issues, and we're ready to go agree to your price—oh, but I have just one small hanging point. We need you to extend the payment terms. You don't have a problem with that, do you?"

As negotiations wind down, it's natural to relax and shift to your back foot. You have emotional equity in the deal, and now you can see the finish line. Maybe you've told your boss it's already done. Besides, you don't want to disappoint your counterpart, your new best friend. Last-minute nibbles can feel manipulative, but are they worth arguing over? What's wrong with conceding if the deal is still good for you?

But here's what you need to consider: It's not really a small concession. Or it's not just one thing but two or three or five. Tactical nibblers will intentionally save a number of requests for the end game, then spring them when you're most vulnerable. Once you extend the payment terms, they'll ask for a smaller down payment. Then some free updates. It's easy to rationalize making any one of these concessions—it won't cost all that much, and you've done it for other customers. Then you add them all up and realize you've been finagled.

Even when the cost seems minimal, nibbling expands the other side's subjective value. That can have a big impact on future negotiations between your organizations.

Here's how to counter:

- Remind yourself that the deal hasn't closed and you're back into bargaining, like it or not. The other side may be belatedly testing your bottom line.

- Whether you wind up acceding to the nibble or not, don't shoot from the hip. Respond reflectively, "I'm going to have to think this over."

- Feel free to flinch hard: "Wait a second, you said we had a deal. This is a whole different ballgame!" Or use an indirect *no*, made famous by businesspeople in Japan: "That would be very difficult." If and when you do give in, the other side will feel more satisfied after hurdling a barrier. And your reluctance may dissuade them from nibbling harder next time.

- Find out if they have more nibbles in mind before agreeing to the first one. Then force their hand by saying, "We'll consider it, but that's *it* now, right?"

- In any subsequent negotiations with a known nibbler, build something extra—a stray goat or chicken—into your position.

Can nibbling ever be legitimate? We'd argue that it's justified under certain conditions:

- You've genuinely overlooked a point that needs to be covered before the deal wraps.

- Conditions have changed over the course of a long negotiation, a common occurrence in construction deals.

- If the seller holds the power and you've been unable to crack their firm price, you might try to get a little extra before the deal is signed. It could be something incremental—a memory upgrade on a mobile device, a one-day-faster delivery. Or you could ask them to throw in some free product, an invisible concession that effectively lowers your cost without eroding the other side's price structure.

Escalation

A friend of ours was selling his small-town Colorado medical practice after getting a big hospital job in Denver. He was asking $350,000 and settled at $325,000, with $50,000 in earnest money until the deal was finalized. On closing day, shortly before his new job was to start, the buyer told him, "I'm sorry, but my father is financing this deal and he feels your practice is only worth $275,000." Faced with the choice of taking a $50,000 haircut or calling off the deal, how do you think our friend responded? That's right, he gulped hard and took the haircut.

It requires considerable negotiating energy and a big psychological investment to bring an agreement to a successful outcome. Then the tension of haggling abates . . . until the other side escalates by reopening a settled issue or raising new ones. They might ask to take back a concession or add on a substantial extra charge. It's nibbling on steroids. Faced with the grim prospect of losing a seemingly done deal, it may seem you have but one way out—to unhappily give in.

Escalation can be borderline unethical, especially at the end of a negotiation. While we don't suggest you use it often, it's good to be prepared to defend against it. In fact, you have options. You might call the other side's bluff and say no. (They don't want to lose the deal either.) You can counter with your own eleventh-hour escalation and insist that they reciprocate. Or, if you can stomach it, you can decide to give in just this once while declaring that you won't allow any further fudging.

Is escalation ever legitimate? Here's one defensible scenario: You're in the middle of a negotiation, and the other party keeps asking for concessions while refusing to budge from their anchor. When all else fails, you might reasonably take back a concession you'd already granted. You're sending a message: You've reached your limit. Some people will keep pushing and pushing until they run into a reality check. An escalation may be your only way to pull them up short.

Number Scrambling

In an episode of *Shark Tank*, two graduate students pitched a proposal for pay-per-use rentals of expensive digital textbooks. Billionaire investor Mark Cuban liked the concept but wasn't satisfied with their offer of 10 percent equity for $200,000. Here's what happened next:

> Entrepreneur #1: Mark, we agree with what you're saying. We want you to be very much vested into PackBack's growth. We would like to offer you 17.5 percent for $200,000.
>
> Cuban: How about $250,000 for 20 percent?
>
> Entrepreneur #1: Would you be willing to do $200,000 for the 20 percent?
>
> Cuban: Yes![6]

Though Cuban took pity and restored the full $250,000 for his 20 percent, the young entrepreneur's flub betrayed his fear of conflict, no doubt heightened by the two sides' power imbalance. It also illustrated the importance of quantifying values. When a discount is requested based on a percentage off list, or the conversation turns to rates per work hour, it can be easy to lose sight of how much money is at stake.

Frank Mobus told the story of a $50 million construction deal where his team was on the selling side. Their standard fee was 12 percent, and the other side was trying to knock it down to 10.5 percent. They were at an impasse when the company president, a fellow named Harold, walked in and asked about the hang-up. The buyer recapped his demand and Harold said, "Take it down a point and a half? Yeah, we can do ten, right, guys?" So where do you think they wound up settling? It was only after a timeout that someone found the nerve to tell Harold that the point and a half would cost them $750,000.

Our automatic system is lousy at math. The moral: never make a concession without calculating beforehand precisely what it's worth.

Identifying Issues Tactics

In bargaining their way to an agreement, there are times when one or both sides have no choice but to move the goalposts. The art is to do it in a way that makes the deal more attractive to the other side.

The Moving Target

You put a kitchen remodel out to bid and your first-choice contractor comes back with a $60,000 proposal. And you say, "That looks great, but I don't have $60,000. The most I can come up with is $50,000—don't blame me, the bank shorted us on our loan."

The contractor doesn't want to lose the job, but he can't meet all the specs and make a decent profit at $50,000. You've effectively pressured him to find ways to take out cost—to go with less expensive cabinet faces, or leave the trim painting to you. But suppose he says, "Look, I've cut every corner, but I still can't do it for less than $60,000."

You say, "All I've got is $50,000, but you know what, my brother is looking for somebody to redo his whole house—that's a kitchen and two bathrooms. If you can do this one for less, maybe I can help you get that one." Now you're not just taking out costs. You're seizing an opportunity to broaden the deal. You're expanding the two sides' total business opportunities, the bridge from advanced bargaining to creative dealmaking.

Summary

- Like poker, bargaining—and especially price haggling—contains an element of gamesmanship and misdirection. But beware of out-and-out deceptions that might undermine your future dealings or business reputation.

- *Take-it-or-leave-it (TIOLI)* is rarely a face-value ultimatum and more often a ploy to build leverage. It works best from a strong power position, and it is usually more effective for buyers (who have more options) than for sellers.

- A buyer's demand for a *best and final offer (BAFO)* can squeeze a seller to close the price gap before the real negotiating even begins. Sellers can deflect a BAFO by preserving room to negotiate and adding points of ambiguity that require a more nuanced discussion.

- *Tactical deadlock* is the ultimate power play, the best way to test the other party's flexibility and resolve—if you can afford to take the risk of losing the deal.

- Be careful and stinting in what you reveal at the bargaining table. An awkward silence can be tactically advantageous. Let the other side blurt out spontaneous disclosures or unplanned concessions while you follow your script and adhere to market norms.

- As a negotiation wraps up, beware of *nibblers* who ask for small, last-minute concessions. You always have the option to grant them or not—or to ask for something in return.

- Before agreeing to a concession, translate percentages and other metrics into real dollars. Make sure you know exactly what you'll be giving up.

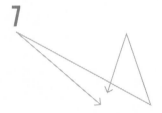

7

Drawing a Map

ADVANCED BARGAINING IN THREE ACTS

Jackson is a sourcing specialist for International Distributors (ID), an import/export company that's in the market for a thin client/server network for 100 users. Lesley is an account manager for High Performance Systems (HPS), a lead bidder.

Information Known to Both Parties

ID sent out a request for proposal with the following specifications:

- Hardware to include user workstations, rack servers, and full fiber-optic network infrastructure

- Additional related services to include: installation, configuration, troubleshooting, technical support, maintenance, and training

- Payment terms are net thirty days

- Delivery and commissioning: thirty days

HPS submitted a total-price bid of $360,000. The company is known for its proficiency in linking to point-of-sale terminals and inventory data. It also went beyond spec to include a manager's dashboard for sales activity, inventory alerts, and key user information, all on one screen.

Information Known Only to the Seller

With an RFP that seemed tailored to her company's strong suits, Lesley is expected to close the sale with ease. Her boss, the regional sales manager, has promised his executive team that it's in the bag. Her boss's boss, the marketing VP, wants the deal badly to open a new market vertical and extend their market reach. The two of them nudge Lesley about it every day. They've given her leeway to offer a 10 percent discount, and she thinks they might okay an additional 5 percent if pushed to the wall. Beyond that it could get dicey, though the executive vice president of sales considers ID a key account. HPS is desperate to cut down on inventory, which is through the roof.

The third quarter ends in three days. HPS sales management is under the gun to get orders on the books, and the pressure is flowing down to Lesley. A month earlier, after whiffing on her last proposal, she heard that she'd lost a half-a-million-dollar deal over a $10,000 price gap. Now she's behind on her quota, her quarterly bonus in jeopardy. Her daughter starts private school next month and the astronomical tuition bill is coming due. Time is of the essence. Her family's Hawaii vacation starts in three days—it's prepaid and can't be canceled. To top everything off, Lesley's backup, who'd step in if the negotiations aren't settled before she leaves, is really bad at his job.

Act One: "You've Got to Do Better Than That"

> Lesley: I think it's pretty straightforward, Jackson. Our proposal covers your department's thin client/server network, client work stations, rack servers, the full fiber network infrastructure, and all related services.
>
> Jackson: Services. That's installation, configuration, trouble-shooting, technical support, maintenance . . .

Lesley: And training.

Jackson: Right. That's the same package everybody is bidding on. And your total price is—wait—is that right? (*He squints down at her proposal and does a theatrical double take.*) You're bidding three hundred and sixty *thousand*?

Lesley: Yes, that's it.

Jackson: (*I bet there's some play in that price.*) Whoo! I've been talking to these other bidders and, Lesley, you're going to have to do better than *that*.

Jackson takes the offensive from the opening gun. HPS is selling a *solution*, a high-tech, high-value product with a host of dedicated services, but Jackson is behaving like a prototypical price haggler. First he tries to commoditize the market: "That's the same package everybody is bidding on." Translation: *Your special features aren't so special. You're the same as everyone else.*

To shake Lesley's confidence and rock her on her back foot, he flinches: "You're bidding three hundred and sixty *thousand*?"

And then Jackson utters the magic words: *You've got to do better than that.* It's a classic price squeeze to test a seller's flexibility and give the buyer more negotiating space. More often than not, it works. Jackson might have resorted to that golden oldie, "You've got to sharpen your pencil." Or the more cryptic, "You're close." We knew a buyer who used that line for years, and he was never technically lying. But here's what no one thought to ask: "Are we close on the high side or the low side?" Some of those sellers were already the low bidders. They wound up bidding against themselves.

When confronted with a price squeeze, a seller's first response is pivotal. The ball is in Lesley's court.

Lesley: How much better am I going to have to do?

Jackson: I can't tell you that, it wouldn't be fair. It's a blind bid. You wouldn't want me to tell the other bidders what your price is, would you?

Lesley: Well, you have to tell me something. If I'm going to do better, I'll need to talk to my boss. I have to know what we're shooting for.

Jackson: Look, I'm only telling you this because I like you, and I want us to do business together. But all I can say is you're going to have to do *significantly* better.

Always seeking a better price, buyers begin with the assumption that most bids are padded. Like Jackson, they're generally reluctant to name a number themselves—what if the seller is ready to go lower than the buyer's estimate? Since most sellers have little faith in their own company's pricing system, they are quick to give ground. As a result, buyers often do well by stonewalling. (At the same time, there's a reciprocation norm at play. When one side shares information, they gain the implicit right to ask for some disclosure in return, as we'll see later on.)

When we left her, Lesley was about to bail on her anchor and plunge right through her floor, a 10 percent discount—her bottom line going in. Most likely her desperation will cost her. First, she's allowed Jackson to pin her to the extreme left of the continuum. When in doubt, buyers fall back on KISS: keep it stupidly simple. But there's no way a quality outfit like HPS can win a raw price war. As the nineteenth-century British writer John Ruskin noted, "There is hardly anything in the world that some man cannot make a little worse and sell a little cheaper."

Lesley needs to nudge the deal into more advanced bargaining, which begins with a simple question: What does the buyer care about *beyond* price alone?

As a general rule, it's ill-advised to answer a buyer's objection before learning its particulars. No price exists in a vacuum. Before making a first concession, Lesley should take some time to find out more about Jackson's needs. It won't be easy, because she's under loads of pressure: her bosses' demands, the quarterly deadline, her imperiled bonus, the beckoning beaches of Oahu, the dreaded school tuition bill. On the other hand, she might stop to consider: Why is Jackson bothering to sit down with her in the first place? Why hasn't he already taken one of those lower bids and run with it?

Here's why: The other side is always under pressure, too.

Information Available Only to the Buyer

Five vendors responded to ID's RFP. All met the basic spec and scope.

- The high bidder came in at $368,000.

- At $360,000, HPS was close to the top.

- Two others came in at $315,000 (12 percent under HPS) and $308,000 (14 percent under). Both indicated an openness to negotiate.

- The low bidder, at $295,000, was a startup with no track record.

Jackson will need his controller to sign off on the purchase, and the ID finance people are telling him, "This is strictly a commodity item. Go with the lowest price." But they said the same thing last year for his big bulk buy from Solid State Drives. The drives were riddled with catastrophic failures and the vendor refused to stand behind them. Jackson's IT contact, Nutley, had warned him to go with another source. Now he rides Jackson about the costly screwup every chance he gets.

On this buy, Nutley prefers HPS. Most ID executives agree. HPS is known for delivering on time. It's the tech leader in its field, a fact that ID could market to its client base. Server downtime is costly, and it's worth paying more to minimize the risk. Finally, Jackson's operations manager is delighted by the dashboard feature. As she's told him more than once, "It shows they really understand our needs."

Jackson hears that HPS usually goes after larger networks. He wonders how badly they want this deal—and how much they'll give in to get it.

Time is tight. After getting sidetracked by two smaller contracts, Jackson no longer has the thirty days specified in the RFP. Now his ops people are saying the network must be up and running in three weeks. Of the three credible bidders besides HPS, Jackson knows that two can't make the new deadline. He doesn't believe the one who says they can.

Now, let's rerun the negotiation from the end of the opening dialogue.

Act Two: "Price Is One Thing; Value Is Another"

Jackson: Whoo! I've been talking to these other bidders and, Lesley, you're going to have to do better than *that*.

Lesley: What do you mean by "better," Jackson—terms? Because net thirty is standard in the industry. Is someone offering better payment terms?

Jackson: Everyone's giving the same terms. Actually, one of the other bidders is offering a quicker install date—he can do it in twenty-one days.

Lesley: I quoted thirty days based on your request. If you need it sooner, I can get it to you sooner. So that's it?

Jackson: No, no—you've got to sharpen your pencil on the price! I've got better bids!

Lesley: Listen, Jackson, we looked closely at your needs and we're offering you a very good deal. Now, I really know this marketplace. I've been in it for a long time. It's hard to believe that anybody has better value than we do.

By prodding Jackson to be more specific, Lesley has learned something. The buyer cares about the installation schedule, which means they're probably under some time pressure. Though Jackson is still trying to drag her back to price, Lesley has begun to carve out some negotiating space of her own.

Jackson: Well, I'm honestly telling you that I've got better prices.

Lesley: Price is one thing; value is another. Why don't we look over the proposal and make sure you understand everything we're offering.

Jackson: Everybody's offering the same thing—same hardware, same software—

Lesley: Same response time? Same availability of parts, of service people?

Jackson: No problem, I've got that covered—everybody's got that.

Lesley: Sure, everybody's got parts, everybody's got people. But where are they located?

Jackson: Located?

Lesley: That's right. Because *where* tells you *when* they're going to show up. Look, here's a map of our locations nationwide. In Pennsylvania, we have two parts depots and one-two-*three* service centers. That means we can get any part to you in less than twenty-four hours—in an emergency, less than six. Are you telling me that everybody's got that?

Jackson: Well, not exactly—

Lesley: Some companies don't have three service centers in the whole country. And you know what happens when you need onsite support? The first thing they do is call their travel agent! And the odds of them having the part you need—well, good luck with that. And what happens when your network fails for eight hours, let alone a second day? What will your operations manager think? And something else you should be thinking about: the quality of people you're working with.

Jackson: Well, no, these are good companies. They have good people.

Lesley: I'm sure they do. But will you be *getting* the good people? Or will they subcontract your service out? You see, HPS is a soup-to-nuts operation. Every one of our people is certified, with a minimum three years' experience. You know, I once lost a customer to a competitor who subbed out his tech support to a specialist. The guy was a wizard with machines. But the first time they had a problem, you know who showed up? The specialist's nephew, a college freshman—a *journalism* major! And listen to this: He forgot to bring the equipment manual!

Jackson: Ohhh, no.

Lesley: Yeah, can you believe it?

What's going on here? Lesley has swung back over her front foot. She's taken control of the narrative with seven pointed words: "Price is one thing; value is another." And she's injected *value mapping,* a valuable tool in both advanced bargaining and an essential one in creative dealmaking. (We'll discuss this in more detail in the next section.) Oftentimes buyers head into a negotiation with a firm sense of their *wants* (chiefly a lower price) but only a vague handle on their *needs.* It falls to the seller to zoom in on those needs and show how the seller's assets can meet them.[1] Sometimes it means showing what they *don't* need in bells and whistles. Sellers know more about the product or service, more about the category, more about the competition. If they're thinking like negotiators, they'll willingly lead the other side through the process.

Lesley goes into detail to show what makes her company the best solution: parts availability, on-time support, service quality. But she doesn't merely list her firm's values in a mechanical way. She attaches each one to a map or anecdote that Jackson can visualize. To gain full credit for the value you're bringing to a deal, it helps to be a good storyteller. When Lesley dramatizes the risk of network downtime, or the college kid who forgot the manual, she's sending a vivid message: *Listen, friend, the same thing could happen to you.*

By establishing her *value proposition,* Lesley is enhancing her bid's value in Jackson's eyes. She's also helping him better understand his own needs—and to sell the deal more effectively within his organization. She's doing him a favor.

At the same time, their price difference remains unresolved. They're still bargaining in their companies' interests; it's still a zero-sum scenario. But with Jackson beginning to see the negotiation in a broader context, a sliver of cooperation creeps into the competition, a shade more transparency. The disagreement takes on a different tone. Both sides are motivated to help the other close the deal.

Act Three: "Is There a Place I Can Make a Call?"

Jackson: Look, you've made some valid points. But still, your price . . .

Lesley: Our price supports our service, and I know that's important to you, Jackson. And our expertise, too. Those lower bids aren't going to be *really* lower. They'll actually cost you more in the long run.

Jackson: But you're so *much* higher than the other bids. Believe me, my financial people will keel over if I give you this order at your quoted price. You've got to come down.

Jackson is stuck in the buyer's dilemma. On the one hand, he's wary of losing a first-rate vendor's values and getting nailed with the consequences. On the other, he's worried that bosses and colleagues will think he's overpaid. Organizational pressure should never be underestimated. Negotiators must satisfy not only the people sitting opposite at the table but also stakeholders who aren't in the room—people like Jackson's controller or Lesley's managers. When planning their negotiation strategy, they'll do well to consider who might have input on the other side. Then they can craft a message—and ultimately an agreement—with those people in mind. Which brings us to our final scene.

Lesley: How much money are we talking about?

Jackson: It's just got to be better than where you came in.

Lesley: Tell you what—why don't you give me a ballpark figure? Come on, Jackson, I really want to help you. But you've got to help me, too. You're not the only one with people looking over their shoulder.

Jackson: Well . . . all right. I'm looking in the neighborhood of $310,000.

Lesley: Three-ten? You're shopping in the wrong neighborhood. If you go with someone at that price, you'll be a hero—until something goes wrong. Then nobody will remember how much money you saved on the initial buy. All they'll talk about is Jackson's disaster.

Jackson: Okay, but you've got to give me *something*, or I'll have people screaming that I gave away the store. If you can't do $310,000, what *could* you do?

Lesley: Is there a place I can make a call?

Jackson: Sure, the conference room is empty, second door on the left.

Though Lesley is ready to close, she sensibly calls timeout. She's not really making that phone call. She has those ten percentage points in her pocket, though she doubts she'll need all ten. She senses she's gained the upper hand. Even so, creative negotiators don't shoot from the hip, even when a deal seems done. It's wiser to step away and ask for a brief caucus or a restroom break—whatever it takes to slow things down and engage our reflective system. A bit of extra time may confirm the wisdom of the move, or refine it. Or maybe a better idea will bubble to the surface. It's all about finding maximum room to maneuver.

On the whole, Lesley did lots of things right. But her performance wasn't quite flawless. A full-blown value proposition has three components—after *mapping* and *illustrating* one's values, the last step is to *quantify* them. Lesley never got around to spelling out just how much a one-day network failure might cost ID. Say that number was $30,000 and Lesley had the data to back it up. Could that have softened Jackson's resistance to her quoted price?

As for Jackson, he was obviously hurt by his lack of preparation. When Lesley had ready comebacks for his haggling tactics, he was left fumbling. By the time he told her he's shooting for something "in the neighborhood of $310,000," Lesley had already shredded his rationale for it. She'd shown that HPS can't be compared to the lower bidders—it's not apples and oranges, it's apples and umbrellas. The buyer was forced to concede that a server network isn't a commodity, after all.

Value isn't a one-way street. Jackson missed an opportunity to establish his own value proposition. He might have tried to leverage his company's prestige value in the industry, its reputation as a prompt payer, and its influence on other divisions in its gigantic parent firm, ID Global. How much might a strong in-house reference be worth to HPS? The lure of future business might have incentivized Lesley to float a larger concession.

Will Jackson and Lesley succeed in closing a deal? The prospects seem promising. Jackson hasn't told Lesley, but he's prepared to pay as much as $340,000. Since Leslie is already authorized to come down as far as $324,000, they have a $16,000 zone of possible agreement (ZOPA). They'll need to keep jousting to decide where they'll land within that overlap. But the fact that they've found a bargaining range at all—after beginning so far apart—is a credit to creative conflict.

Summary

- When you're feeling under stress to sell out your target price, take a breath and remind yourself: *The other side's under pressure, too.*

- A price squeeze is a classic buyer's ploy to test a seller's flexibility. In advanced bargaining, the seller counters by broadening the deal beyond price alone and showing the *value* they bring to the table.

- Before making the first concession, use your discovery skills to learn more about the other party's needs. If they've criticized your proposal or your company, press them for details. By learning more, you may be able to satisfy their concerns without moving off your price.

- It's not enough to recite a laundry list of assets. For maximum impact, you need to attach them to persuasive narratives and then quantify them.

- Most deals have a ZOPA, a zone of possible agreements. Creative negotiators collaborate to find that common ground and then compete to close at a number that's favorable to their side.

Part Three

THE TRADER
(CREATIVE DEALMAKING)

Value mapping   Complex collaborating

8

Moving around the Table

Ron works in purchasing for a medium-sized merchandising chain that battles the Goliaths of the consumer electronics sector. A few years back, he was thrown for a loss when Walmart and its Asian supplier made an exclusive deal for clock radios, one of Ron's critical categories, at a subterranean price point. Soon Walmart was dominating the market. Ron's company was getting killed.

But Ron is resourceful, and he found a Taiwan manufacturer with a better price. Unfortunately, it was still 20 percent too high to compete with Walmart. Both sides wracked their brains to take out cost. Modify the performance specs? Go cheaper on packaging? Streamline shipping and logistics? Finally, the manufacturer said, "Look, if I go any further, there's no margin for me." The price Ron needed would push them below their cost of production.

"I thought that was the end of the road," Ron told us. "I just couldn't see any way to make this deal." But then he thought some more about how negotiating changes as we move along the continuum. In bargaining, we ask ourselves: *How can I drive the other side to its bottom line?* In dealmaking, we shift from the tactical to the strategic: *What does the other side need that they might not have considered?* And: *Can I meet their needs by opening new possibilities in the deal?*

So Ron set price aside—for the moment—and started thinking like a negotiator. He'd noticed how quiet the Taiwan plant had seemed that summer. After asking the supplier several complicated questions, now he posed a simple one: "What's your production cycle?"

And the man replied, "In the summer, things are really slow. We have to shut down one of our three assembly lines and lay off a quarter of our workforce. Then we hire back in the fall."

Ron said, "And when you rehire, do your old workers come back?"

"Yes and no. The best ones—maybe 20 percent—find other jobs." That meant hiring new people each September, training them, and restarting the dormant assembly line, an added expense unto itself. Even then, the new workers weren't as efficient as the experienced people the manufacturer had lost. All in all, the transition cost was hundreds of thousands of dollars each year.

That's when Ron saw the light. "What if you produced our entire order during your slow season, and then we warehoused the inventory until we need them? If you could keep your good workers, wouldn't that save you more than a 20 percent discount?"

It sure would! Since Ron's company had abundant warehousing capacity, they could accept one big annual delivery without strain. Most important, they got the price they needed to compete. Meanwhile, the Taiwan supplier found a way to keep all of their production lines up and running year-round. They took a per-unit loss on each clock radio and still came out ahead.

Ron's solution stepped past advanced bargaining. He did more than target one-way concessions; his source went beyond trimming fat from their bid. The two sides *traded* concessions to *expand* the deal and find *mutual* opportunities. They found new things to negotiate that hadn't been on the table. They created a ZOPA where none previously existed. Though the final price was the same number that once had them at an impasse, its meaning had changed. The two sides wound up creating value that exceeded the sum of its parts.

Equally important, they developed an unanticipated relationship. Their interactions became more relaxed and constructive. As Kahneman points out, "Negotiations over a shrinking pie are especially difficult, because they require an allocation of losses. People tend to be much more easygoing when they bargain over an expanding pie."[1]

On a small scale, Ron's story reflects the transformative potential of a creative approach to conflict.

Going to the Next Level

Einstein once said, "No difficult problem can be solved at its own level; it has to be looked at in a more complex way." When are we compelled to break through to creative dealmaking? When bargaining reaches its limits. Buyers can get only so far by pounding suppliers on price. If a gap remains and the seller can't or won't move any further, conventional price pushing leaves one of two unsavory choices: make a big concession or abandon the deal.

Creative dealmakers aren't so easily boxed in. When tactics fall short, they take a more strategic tack—to define their needs and to generate new business opportunities. But they cannot do it alone. To pursue the third way, both sides must reconsider the deal in a collaborative fashion. They need to migrate to the edge of the inside to better understand what matters to the other party. They're not just hearing people out, they're absorbing their concerns as their own.

Human beings are natural value producers. As we shift to the other party's side of the table, we begin to view the problem from a similar angle. Our focus turns from contention to the need for a solution—from what divides us to what might unite us. The dealmaking arena offers several advantages:

- By giving people more to talk about, it expands negotiating space and lends more room to maneuver.

- By narrowing the gap between perspectives, it softens the tone of disagreement and reduces tension.

- By thinking outside of the bargaining box, negotiators open the deal to new value-creating possibilities.

Where bargaining is driven by adversarial competition and conflicting positions, creative dealmaking looks at the two parties' *interests* and how they might fit together. What are the other side's deeper needs, including ones they may not even be aware of?

What assets do we have to meet them, and vice versa? And amid this constellation of assets and needs, what are the complementary tradeoffs that might vault us into a more ambitious deal? In a time when products and services have so many moving parts, the potential value of this approach has grown exponentially. But we repeat: to unlock those opportunities, you'll need a two-sided outlook and the freedom to color outside the lines.

Creative dealmaking is a tightrope. It rests on the knife's edge, the point where competition and cooperation have equal weight. While the balance is tricky, the payoffs can be huge. We're no longer content with an incremental gain—we're looking to leapfrog our rivals and disrupt the market, to find mutual gain synergies that might catapult both sides to the top of their fields. In today's wildly mercurial economy, companies need more than hardnosed bargainers to survive. Winning a few percentage points is necessary but no longer sufficient. Creative negotiators are in vogue like never before.

Let's examine a case where two household names found a creative solution that changed the lives of business travelers the world over.

A Better Cup of Joe

Some years ago, a United Airlines passenger survey drove one point home: Airplane coffee was horrible. The survey caught the eye of a sales executive at Starbucks, then a medium-sized company with six hundred stores but no international presence. In an effort to raise their profile, Starbucks invited United to go where no airline had gone before, to serve first-rate coffee at thirty-five thousand feet. United was eager to improve their customer service and distinguish their brand from Delta and American. The two sides started talking.

For Starbucks, the deal had tremendous upside. United flew 2,200 flights a day and ranked as the largest US carrier to Europe and Asia. One of four United passengers asked for coffee, which meant twenty million potential customers a year.

But for a young, unproven company, one that lived or died by quality control, there was downside risk as well. The taste of water varied from city to city. Onboard brewing equipment could be erratic. And it was easy to picture a harried flight attendant leaving a pot sitting longer than twenty minutes, the strict limit at Starbucks shops. What if people's first impression of their coffee was awful?

Then there was the issue of pricing. Starbucks normally cost more than twice as much as brand X, and United wanted them to do better—a *lot* better. When Starbucks submitted its bid, United shot it down. If they paid that much, it would blow their whole cost structure! They disclosed their coffee budget, a number that would lose Starbucks money on every cup.

In most cases, it's at that point where negotiations break down. Each party tells itself, "Good idea, nice try, but the gap is too wide." When you're too far apart to plausibly split the difference, price bargaining hits a wall. The deal dies.

But creative negotiators don't relent so easily. United's executives kept asking themselves: What are Starbucks' broader interests? What do they *really* need?"

The airline broke the deadlock by proposing an ingenious trade-off. First, Starbucks would divert half its modest advertising budget to help cover a markdown on inflight coffee. In return, United would feature the Seattle-based brand in a high-profile national run of print, radio, and TV ads—exposure that Starbucks couldn't dream of affording at the time. And here was the clincher: Every beverage trolley in every United plane would be adorned with Starbucks stickers and piled with cups bearing the Starbucks logo.

The deal had changed. United's sweeteners enlarged the value pie. Like Ron's clock radio supplier, Starbucks could sell each unit of its product at a loss and still come out ahead. And if they gave it their best shot and it didn't work out? Well, millions of prospective new customers were worth rolling those dice.

Motivated like never before, Starbucks created a training course for United flight attendants on how to brew superior coffee. A new quality assurance program set the optimal "dosage" and grind for each pot. After rigorously testing the airline's brewing apparatus, they prevailed upon United to keep a pricey stainless steel part instead of replacing it on the cheap. The goal, according to Starbuck's chief marketing officer, was to enlarge the brand's potential "while keeping its integrity and soul intact."[2] Internally, the company launched a digital manufacturing system to boost efficiency by 30 percent, which made their discount to United easier to swallow. By that point, the deal had grown more transformative than either side could have foreseen at the start.

Less than one year after the fateful customer survey, a new United ad campaign rolled out on the back covers of *BusinessWeek*, *Time*, and *U.S. News & World Report*. It featured a Styrofoam cup with the Starbucks logo, and a tagline: "We're about to give airplane coffee a good name." And at the bottom of the page: "United is now serving Starbucks coffee on every flight worldwide."

Within three months, 71 percent of United passengers were rating their coffee as good or excellent. Fourteen percent said it was the first time they'd tried Starbucks. United Chairman and CEO Glenn Tilton credited the coffee company with helping to propel the airline's customer satisfaction to "historically high levels."[3]

Four years after the two companies joined forces, Starbucks had more than three thousand stores and vaulted into the S&P 500. It had penetrated Tokyo, Beijing, Seoul, and Hong Kong, traditional tea-drinking capitals that happened to be served by United. To this day, the Far East remains Starbucks' fastest-growing market. By 2018, the company was opening a new store in China every fifteen hours.[4] Here's a trivia question: Which city boasts the most Starbucks outlets in the world?

The answer: Seoul, South Korea.[5]

Starbucks' historic runaway success owes to brilliant branding, sustained category leadership, and a trove of strategic partnerships—with Barnes and Noble, PepsiCo, Breyer's Ice Cream, Kraft, and Apple. But the company's early triumph with United shows how a little creative conflict can go a long, long way.

The Limits of KISS

In our buy/sell exercise for the artisanal pizza oven, we furnish both sides with briefing sheets that could guide them to mutual gain tradeoffs. They might consider a joint marketing plan to leverage the oven's brand value; on-site training by the oven-maker's brother, a master baker of breakfast breads in Italy; an extended warranty the seller could offer without qualms, since their product was built to last forever; a commitment to buy additional ovens as the buyer builds out a local chain.

Yet nine times out of ten, our practice negotiators remain stuck in zero-sum haggling. Opportunities for added value—for potential *bonanzas*—go begging. It's like an O. Henry story. Though each side has something of high value to the other, their mutual suspicions choke off more creative solutions.

Why are people so reluctant to align for a superior deal? For starters, empathy is hard work. Creative dealmaking makes negotiating more complicated. It soaks up time and energy, two precious commodities in business. Moreover, there's no guarantee it will work out in the end. If you find negotiating painful, you'll want to get in and out of it as quickly and simply as you can.

A second reason is tied to our mental models. When disagreements flare, our automatic system spotlights the conflict. Those fight-or-flight chemicals kick in. We raise our defenses and hunker down in fixed positions—our so-called comfort zone. Since transparency makes us feel more vulnerable, we go into a shell. We lose our capacity to address our deeper needs or how the other side might meet them, much less how to go out of our way to aid our adversary. The fears that make bargaining so unpleasant also disable our creativity, the very thing we need to make it *less* onerous. We're trapped in one-sided competition, a one-way street into the dead end of antagonism.

William Anton refers to the "small circle" of how we function day to day, based on our mental models, and the far larger circle of our untapped potential:

> *Competition* is the process that occurs between two people or groups operating as small circles trying to gain an advantage

over the other. *Pursuing excellence*, on the other hand, is the process of reducing the gap between the large and small circles. Ironically, the individuals and organizations that pursue excellence tend to have a competitive advantage over others.[6]

But how to move into those larger circles when competition is ever present? In other words: How can we make conflict more creative?

Trust and Vigilance

In a meta-analysis of negotiation studies, Stuart Diamond found that the substance of the deal amounted to only a sliver—as little as 8 percent—of the basis for agreements. A little more than one-third related to process: agendas, discovery, commitments. The main driver of agreement? The two parties' mutual affinity.[7] The make-or-break factor was how much we liked and trusted the person sitting on the other side.

Negotiating is fraught because it makes us interpret—or guess at—what our opposite number is really saying. Say I'm the buyer and I tell you, "That's all I've got in my budget, so I need you to help me." In creative dealmaking, that's an oft-used collaborative tactic to broaden the deal. On the other hand, my motive might be more opportunistic—to attack your price and test your flexibility. My limited budget could be a bargaining subterfuge, a ruse to get you to tip your hand and collapse to your bottom line.

Traditional negotiating courses go by a time-honored rule: *Don't trust.* In business, after all, you can rarely be sure of whom you *can* trust. Strangers are wild cards by definition. Even if you know the other party, their intent may be cloudy, even to themselves. Since we can't be certain as to when they're bluffing or withholding (or even lying), we're taught that it's safest to assume they're out to get you at all times.

But while an on-guard outlook might sound pragmatic and street-smart, it's at best a distortion of reality. There *are* predators out there, to be sure, people who will stop at nothing to gain maximum leverage, but they're in the small minority. Most people aren't like that. Approaching everyone on a *don't trust* basis hurts our long-term interests. A talented entrepreneur once told us, "I know very few people I could trust over the course of a lifetime—no one, in fact." Despite his ambition and hard work, his business stopped growing. He was hobbled by suspicion, which in turn made him suspect to others. His wary social style eventually ground him to a halt.

Creative negotiators aren't reckless. They don't usher strangers into the tent with open arms. But they exchange *don't trust* for a more balanced stance: *Be vigilant.* By looking out for themselves while also seeking opportunities, they're positioned to make bigger, better deals. They'll share more information and take some *calculated* risk. Rather than prejudge the other party, they assess their behavior and respond accordingly. Some people will prove to be more scrupulous than others, and some will be more aggressive than others. As long as our eyes stay open and our ears are close to the ground, we'll be able to protect our interests.

As added value is created and negotiations grow less adversarial, the natural tendency is to assume the other person will be fair in sharing the rewards. But don't be lulled. No matter how friendly the process, creative dealmaking relies on reciprocating and *matching*, not unconditional giving. Like everything else, trust must be continuously negotiated.

Yes and No

We live in a culture where *no* is a difficult word to hear. It's painful to us as to infants, and it never loses its sting—it's that social norm of ours, rearing its head. We hate hearing *no* and hate to disappoint others by saying it. *Yes*, on the other hand, quells the anxiety of disagreement. That's one reason why Fisher and Ury's landmark *Getting to Yes* resonated with so many people, though often for the wrong reasons.

At the bargaining table, it's the easiest thing in the world to say "yes," assuming you have the flexibility to meet the other side's requests. But here's the inconvenient truth: *No* is the essence of negotiating, the fount of creative conflict. Nothing kills a deal's potential like a premature *yes*. As Karrass veteran Mel Klayman would say, "Look, don't just agree with me. It's too soon. There's more in here!" Where *yes* ends the process, *no* keeps it alive to hunt for hidden assets and unexpressed needs. It forces the two sides to invest more time together and deepen their relationship. In creative dealmaking, *no* does the heavy lifting.

In a sense, the art of negotiating lies in saying no while keeping the conversation going. Depending on the circumstances and the mood in the room, there are many ways to get the message across without putting off the other party. You can say no theatrically, with a flinch thrown in for good measure. You can say, "No, but . . ." in the spirit of discovery. Only in extreme cases does *no* mean *never*. More often it signifies *not yet* or *not exactly* or simply, *tell me more*. A willingness to say no—not just once, but repeatedly—will make your ultimate *yes* more confident and satisfying. You'll avoid the what-might-have-been regrets that haunt many a superficially successful outcome.

What we're after, as Richard Rohr put so well, is "to balance the small bubble in the glass between here and there, between yes and no . . . [and] hold these perspectives in a necessary creative tension."[8] That bubble is a sphere of uncertainty but also great potential. It's the place where we truly start thinking like negotiators.

No and *yes* are the yang and yin of negotiating, a pair of intertwined opposites. They're the source code for the conflict that drives the creative process. As Ury himself came to realize, "Yes without No is appeasement, whereas No without Yes is war."[9] To which we'd add: *No* is where creative dealmaking begins.

Beyond Win-Win

In 1980, IBM boasted the largest market cap of any corporation in the world. Dominant in mainframe computers, it was *the* technology behemoth. In a fast-tracked venture into personal computers, which were just taking off, it contracted with a young, privately held software company out of Seattle to create a new operating system. To ward off the specter of antitrust suits, IBM drafted a nonexclusive deal. The Seattle firm would still own its software and be allowed to license the system to other manufacturers— because who, after all, could compete with Big Blue? Besides, IBM got a great price. The system cost them just $45,000.[10]

When the state-of-the-art IBM PC came out the following year, it took the tech world by storm. By 1985, it was the market leader. IBM was over the moon. So was the Seattle software firm, busy selling its DOS (disk operating system) to copy-cat clones and using the PC as a launchpad for more sophisticated programs. A classic win-win, right?

Flash forward to the mid-1990s. IBM is floundering. With the explosive rise of personal computers and client servers, mainframes look like the dinosaurs just after the asteroid struck. Meanwhile, the IBM PC has been lapped by cheaper facsimiles from Compaq and Dell. By 1998, that obscure software company in a remote corner of the country—now public and all grown up— doubled IBM's market cap. As of January 2021, Microsoft was the second-largest company in the world, behind only Apple. It was valued at more than 1.6 *trillion* dollars, or close to fifteen times the not-so-Big Blue.

Let's return to the 1980 agreement that put all those wheels into motion. Was it really a win-win? Or was it a win-lose, or something in between?

The now-iconic concept of win-win derived from Fisher and Ury's concept of principled negotiation, as charted in *Getting to Yes* (2011). It represented a big advance, a more flexible and strategic approach to making deals. But over the years, as win-win became part of our general lexicon, it became watered down into an insipid soup at the bargaining table. It was how they might have negotiated in Garrison Keillor's Lake Wobegon, "where all the women are strong, all the men are good-looking, and all the children are above average." Whenever two sides made a quick-and-dirty compromise, often by splitting the difference, they left the table subjectively pleased with the deal. They felt like winners because they'd surpassed their low expectations going in. Or maybe they'd panicked over a looming impasse and were grateful to settle for anything. Either way, win-win became a euphemism for settling cheap and giving in.

In our pizza oven exercise, where the asking price is $95,000, 25 percent of our negotiating pairs settle between $90,000 and $94,000. That's a not-so-hot outcome for the buyer, since the seller's bottom line is around $70,000, the sum they need to repay their bank loan and avoid a forced liquidation. Half of our pairs settle between $85,000 and $90,000—call it an average deal. The remaining 25 percent land between $76,000 and $85,000, a superior deal for the buyer.

When we ask the top-performing quartile of buyers to rate their satisfaction, they're happy, as you might expect—around 9 on a scale of 1 to 10. Then we survey the lowest-performing group, who know by then how the other buyers fared and how low their seller might have gone. Their average satisfaction score? A strongly positive 8.5. By any objective measure, they'd been fleeced in a lopsided transaction—and yet they still came out feeling like winners. It's enough to make a manager cynical. As one of our client companies told us, "The way our strategic partners use 'win-win' is that they try to win twice and leave us holding the bag."

As we see it, win-win fails on two counts. First, it dismisses the friction that negotiators need to succeed. Creative dealmaking isn't a warm and fuzzy kumbaya chorus. Even when you've managed to create added value, the negotiation doesn't scream to a halt. You still need to *quantify* the value you've created, then decide how the two sides will share it. Those mutually lucrative tradeoffs still have to be worked back into a contract price. The competitive piece of creative conflict—where one party's gain comes at the other's cost—remains alive and well. And whenever there's competition, as we know, there are winners and losers.

Does this mean the two sides may at times revert to bargaining? Yes, but with an asterisk. If the process unspooled as it should, their bond will be stronger than before. Their interplay will be different than a narrowly focused, value-splitting price battle. Instead of degenerating into angry argument, the energy of conflict—of openly voiced differences—will be channeled into solving the problem at a higher level. Because no matter how sharp the disagreement, it's not just a *bigger* pie that's getting shared. It's the difference between a cornstarch-and-preservative special from the corner grocery and your grandmother's homemade specialty on her best day. It's a *better* pie.

The second fatal weakness of win-win? When you get down to it, there's no way to know who's won at the moment the contract is inked. Deals are made according to estimates of the market, but it's hard to tell where the market should be. The agreement we make today isn't exactly what it will be when executed next month or next year. Most quantifiers are probabilistic at best. They rely on projected growth and the prospect of future business between the two sides, as well as unpredictable shifts in the macroeconomic climate. Given all the variables, it can be very hard to judge whether a deal is truly fair.

We're not declaring IBM the loser in its deal for an operating system. PC-DOS served its needs well, at least in the short run. But with the passage of time, it's clear that this wasn't an even-steven, win-win affair. At best it was win-*WIN*, with Microsoft grabbing the lion's share of created value. Thanks to Windows 10, DOS's great-great-grandbaby and a cash cow par excellence, Microsoft is still reaping that share to this day.

But if winning is a guesstimate, and fairness itself subjective, what can we say with assurance about creative dealmaking? Simply this: win-win doesn't meet our standard. Placid compromises aren't good enough. Stubborn price haggling doesn't make the grade, either. Without an effort to advance along the continuum, to move beyond zero-sum bargaining and probe for more creative solutions, the outcome is often *lose-lose*. (We'd argue that most of our pairs in the pizza oven exercise achieve exactly that.)

We believe you can create a better deal, not just a better feeling. A deal that adds objective value for *both* sides. Once you arrive there, you can act strategically to nail down a healthy share of the bounty . . . or maybe a little more.

In the following chapter, we'll show you how to do just that.

Summary

- In creative dealmaking, the two parties find reciprocal tradeoffs to expand the deal—and often to forge a new ZOPA where none seemed to exist.

- By focusing on solutions rather than points of division, the continuum's middle mode expands negotiating space, reduces tension, and nurtures creative conflict.

- Mutual gain synergies contain the power to disrupt whole industries.

- Creative dealmakers stand ready to trust the other side, as warranted, but remain vigilant in protecting their own interests.

- *No* is the most indispensable word in negotiating—not to shut down the process but to keep it going in pursuit of a better, more creative deal.

- Win-win is a myth. It ignores the reality that the two sides are still competing for the larger share of any added value, even in a deal that's better for both sides.

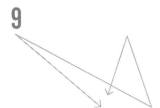

9

Creative Dealmaking

STRATEGIES AND TACTICS

NBC was between a rock and a hard place. It was 1998, and they had no professional football in their lineup. After vowing not to sign any more sports rights deals that would leave them in the red, they were on the outside looking in. "We made a cold, calculated decision that the losses were intolerable," said Dick Ebersol, chairman of NBC Sports.[1]

The call made financial sense, but it hurt. NBC pioneered the first televised National Football League game in 1939. It televised the first Super Bowl. Now the once-dominant peacock was sorely missing an anchor to promote its new fall shows. Seven years after the network opted out, the NFL put up for bid a new six-year contract for *Sunday Night Football*. NBC's ratings were tanking, and it desperately wanted back in the game. The problem was the league's sticker-shock asking price: $3.6 billion for a six-year package, or $600 million annually—about $150 million more than projected advertising revenues.[2] The gap was too large to be closed with transactional bargaining. There was no conceivable way to split the difference and meet in the middle. The situation seemed hopeless.

That's when Ebersol and Jeff Zucker, chief executive of parent company General Electric's (GE) NBC Universal Television

Group, started thinking like negotiators. Modeling their approach after NBC's agreement with the International Olympic Committee, they brainstormed on how to expand the deal. Where could more value be generated? What did GE sell that the NFL might need?

As it turned out, quite a lot. GE's new security services unit could serve the stadiums on game day. GE Medical Products Company could provide onsite healthcare technology. GE Finance could enlarge the company's existing stake in a leaguewide loan pool for new stadium construction. And then there were all the lightbulbs that made those dramatic night games *pop*—tens of millions of watts of lightbulbs. Altogether, the non-TV businesses could add $500 million in sales, more than enough to cover the ad revenue shortfall and net a substantial profit. General Electric CEO Jeff Immelt green-lit the deal.

"It's just innovative business," Zucker said after the contract was signed. "It's innovative deal making."[3] By shifting from bargaining to creative dealmaking, GE and the NFL found a novel way to match assets and needs. Their transformative agreement forever changed the landscape for major league rights negotiations. We don't know who won the deal—that's a distribution issue, and a complex one at that. But here's what we do know: The two parties found a solution that was indisputably better for both of them.

The Fork in the Road

Whenever negotiators are at loggerheads, they come to a fork in the road. One path—the straight and narrow one—takes them to the place of concessions and givebacks. Both sides end up with *less* than what they'd wanted. The second path, the more winding and elusive one, leads to a land where both sides get *more* than they'd bargained for. In a nutshell, that's the difference between bargaining and creative dealmaking. The game shifts from a contest to a shared mission: *How can we restructure this deal to our mutual benefit?*

As we tilt away from competition and toward cooperation, the five basic strategies of bargaining change as well:

- **Leverage building** moves from purely *consequential* leverage (to make the other side fear the repercussions if they don't fall in line and compromise) to a mix of consequential and *positive* leverage, where they're incentivized to collaborate to get more out of the deal. It's the difference between the stick and the carrot.

- **Discovery** shifts from an effort to exploit the other side's vulnerabilities to a dialogue that surfaces hidden aspects of the deal, often outside the RFP. Both sides share information to promote a better understanding of their assets and needs.

- **Target-setting** evolves from a numbers game to setting broader goals that align with the other side's values. For example, one of our clients, a major consumer electronics supplier, targeted a 7 percent price increase. Then they realized they could get a much better deal by *cutting* their price hike to 5 percent. In return, the retailer agreed to stock more of their items, improve their shelf space and displays, and cross-promote their flagship product in advertising circulars.

- **Concession-making** turns from the quest for one-sided concessions to trades of concessions of comparable subjective value—a.k.a. the quid pro quo. While creative dealmakers are freer than bargainers in offering concessions, they still make the other side work for them, if only to increase the recipient's satisfaction.

- **Identifying issues** moves from shaving cost to *value mapping*, where the two sides determine how best to work together to add value and broaden the deal.

The Alpha Dog: Value Mapping

In this middle mode of the continuum, the strategies also have a different order of importance. Where leverage building leads the way in bargaining, the skeleton key for creative dealmaking is value mapping. In contrast to pricing, value is essentially subjective—it's colored by the parties' circumstances. In both the Starbucks/United and NFL/NBC deals, negotiators found a way to alter the *meaning* of the price without touching the raw numbers. They made the leap from total cost of ownership to total business opportunities, which includes the potential for more comprehensive deals in the future. By transcending business as usual, they uncovered mutual gain tradeoffs and a new deal that was better for both sides.

Like 3D binoculars, value mapping enables us to see a negotiation in a more penetrating way. What additional (and affordable) assets do you have that I might value more than you do? What assets do *I* have to meet your needs, even ones you may be unaware of? It's all about gauging our asymmetries and how they could dovetail. To paraphrase Adam Grant, creative dealmakers take a conditional, negotiating giver approach to matching. We're channeling conflict into a superior outcome.

In bargaining, where we're trying to claim as much value as we can, a weak opponent can be profitably exploited. But in creative dealmaking, we actually do better when the other side is skilled and savvy enough to help find extra opportunities. When dealing with less experienced counterparties, it can be to our advantage to guide them through the process. Salespeople, in particular, shouldn't assume that a buyer fully understands what they have on offer. Even when they can't budge on price, creative negotiators can enhance their product's subjective value. By painting a vivid picture of an item's features, they deepen the buyer's appreciation for how it might help them. *Consultative sellers* take this one step further. Instead of presuming that one size fits all, they engage on the customers' turf, analyze their problems, and arrive at customized solutions.

In principle, value mapping is straightforward. Say an office supply retailer needs a bulk order of high-end walnut desk sets. The supplier offers to distribute them to the buyer's stores. Since the seller uses their own trucks, it costs them only $5 per unit while saving the buyer $15 per unit in carrier fees. In exchange, the cash-flush buyer agrees to pay in full upon delivery, which saves the seller $15 per unit in financing costs. The tradeoff enlarges the total value pie by $25 per unit [($15–$5) + $15]. Both sides come out ahead, though the buyer does slightly better on paper than the seller. Alternatively, for a similar premium, the seller might agree to deliver in ten days instead of three weeks. Or they might agree to throw in a free upgrade in exchange for entree to other business within the buyer's organization. The possibilities are endless.

Forging a Value Proposition

In the planning runup to value mapping, creative negotiators build their *value proposition* in three stages:

- *Mapping* values to connect our assets to the other side's needs and vice versa. Going into a negotiation, it helps to make two lists—the concessions you want, and what you're willing to give up to get them.

- *Illustrating* values with narrative devices to show how we can help the other side. The ideal is a persuasive story, not a rigid last word: "This is my best guess right now, and I think it's the right answer, but I'm open to other opinions."

- *Quantifying* values to make benefits more tangible by estimating their worth for both parties. (If there's disagreement over the numbers, a clean-sheet or should-cost analysis can often resolve it.)

While value propositions are traditionally deployed by sellers, buyers can leverage them as well. Consider the added-value items a savvy purchaser can bring to a deal: cash upfront, branding value and prestige, referrals to other corporate divisions, higher-volume orders, growth and future business, reliable on-time payment, low-maintenance deal management.

We do significant work with the energy industry, which periodically struggles with down markets. Here's a typical scenario: A production manager from an oil major like ExxonMobil or Shell is negotiating the lease of a drilling rig with an account manager from Horizon or Nabors. Because of pricing pressures outside of either party's control, there is no apparent ZOPA. The production manager starts by bringing down the hammer and anchoring low: "We're shelving projects right and left. If you want to work with us, you'll need to lower your price at least 30 percent."

And the account manager responds, "I can't get even close to that—it's way below my cost. Fifteen percent is my bottom line."

Let's stipulate that neither side is bluffing or playing games. The buyer is being genuine when he says, "Then we'll probably just cancel this project."

But hold the phone! Once the two parties see that they can't make a deal by squeezing out another 5 percent or so, there's just one way to meet their objectives and placate their internal stakeholders. They need to make a different kind of agreement. In this case, the buyer might say, "The only way I can settle for 15 percent off is if you upgrade the rig to the one with your latest technology."

The seller comes back with, "I can do that if you pay me half upfront. And I'd need you to start within three months, to get some revenue flowing."

The buyer responds, "I should be able to manage that—if you can guarantee that you'll put your best people on the job."

The seller says, "That's easy! And you know what? Now that I'm thinking about it, I might be able to wangle a better price if we can share some of the revenue."

By the time the negotiators are done, they've worked out a whole new deal—one that exceeds their original objectives. Had they tried to haggle their way through, odds are they would have deadlocked and gotten no deal at all.

The challenge of creative dealmaking is to know *where* to mine for the subtle, hidden values inherent in every exchange. Since they may be overlooked in the heat of a high-stress negotiation, it's wiser not to rely on inspiration in the moment. A value mapping checklist is an essential planning tool. The generic version below can get you started, but it's better to create a customized checklist for each transaction. As you'll see, the scope of potential tradeoffs is bound only by the two parties' creativity.

VALUE MAPPING CHECKLIST

- **Payment terms.** When one side has ready access to financing or is cash-rich, and the other side's cash flow is tight, a change in payment terms can render a low-cost, high-value benefit. *Possibilities*: extended payment period for larger orders, less (or more) money down, stretched progress payments, a larger retention pending final approval.

- **Delivery schedule.** A certain schedule may be valuable to one side and indifferent to the other. *Possibilities*: shorter lead times, faster delivery.

- **Warranty.** If the supplier is confident that their product will function as specified with a low failure rate, and the purchaser is nervous on both counts, a warranty can be a high-value sweetener. *Possibilities*: extended warranty, express warranty for repair or replacement within a set timeframe.

- **Packaging can be customized to fit a buyer's needs and make the item ready for immediate shipment to end users.** *Possibilities*: supplying a mixed assortment of goods per pallet, simplified packaging by shipping in bulk.

- **Transportation and logistics.** One side or the other may have underutilized capacity for shipping. Say the seller has half-empty trucks that pass by the purchaser's warehouses. Or one side or the other may have a more favorable agreement with a third-party logistics outfit. *Possibilities*: a break on volume shipping costs, delivery to one central location versus a number of satellite destinations.

- **Order size.** When initial setup is a major cost component, and extra production is relatively inexpensive, larger orders will sharply reduce unit costs. If the purchaser has excess storage space plus easy access to financing, the extra inventory is no great burden. On the other hand, if the item is close to obsolescence or sales are uncertain, upping the order may be too great a risk.

- **Inventory adjustment.** A purchaser stands to benefit from late order adjustments to correspond to fluctuating inventory. A key factor is the seller's flexibility for altering their output. *Possibilities*: consignment sales, where the buyer pays the seller as goods are used; vendor-managed inventory, where the buyer shares inventory data and the seller defines order size.

- **Timing.** In seasonal industries (think: Christmas trees), shipping and delivery are keyed to special times of the year. The timing will often hinge on what fits best the companies' other business lines. Is there a low season when the seller's facilities would otherwise sit idle?

- **Specification changes.** Some specifications can be tweaked to suit either or both parties. In some cases, a spec can be simplified to take out cost while still guaranteeing the customer what they need. In others, it may be upgraded to give the buyer more functionality, reliability, or ease of assembly at a marginal price increase.

- **Joint effort.** Creative dealmakers commonly collaborate to cuts costs and raise quality, either in a one-time effort or a pilot program for a full-blown partnership. *Possibilities*: design tweaks, coordinated ordering process.

- **Quality control.** The features that matter most to the purchaser are often low-impact variables for the seller/manufacturer. Sellers often can assure high quality control on these issues without significantly raising production costs. *Possibilities*: allowing purchaser inspections during manufacturing, agreeing to accept returns that fall short of the standard.

- **Shifting resources.** Who does what for whom? Say it's an order for motorcycle frames. Can additional processes—like painting or heat-treating—be passed off to the supplier? On the flip side, can the customer take on additional work inhouse? *Possibility*: the customer has the ability to buy raw materials at a lower price than the supplier.

- **Cooperative marketing/advertising.** Like United and Starbucks, the two parties advertise both of their firms and/or products at the same time. *Possibilities:* cross-promotional packaging, joint media ad campaigns, joint marketing at trade shows, sporting event partnerships, sharing product roadmaps and lifecycle information.

- **Extra services.** Again, the value to one side may vastly exceed the cost to the other. *Possibilities:* installation support, a service contract, onsite engineering, dedicated customer service reps, testing, training.

- **Data is the quintessential low-cost, high-benefit sweetener.** Beyond adding immediate financial value, transparent sharing of information can strengthen a longer-term relationship. *Possibilities*: product roadmaps, market intelligence, technology updates, timely notification of upcoming changes, feedback on newly available products.

Connect for Success

Life is about discovering the right questions more than having the right answers.
—**Richard Rohr**

Advanced bargaining helps us solve problems, primarily our own. When a good price alone won't cut it, we imagine other ways to make a deal work for our organization. In creative dealmaking, the challenge is more complex. Daniel Pink explains:

> The services of others are far more valuable when I'm mistaken, confused, or completely clueless about my true problem. In those situations, the ability to move others hinges less on problem *solving* than on problem *finding*. . . .

> After all, my ultimate aim isn't to acquire a vacuum cleaner. It's to have clean floors. Maybe my real problem is that the screens on my windows aren't sufficient to keep out dust. . . . Maybe my problem is that my carpet collects dirt too easily, and a new carpet will obviate the need for me to always be vacuuming. . . . Maybe there's an inexpensive cleaning service with its own equipment that serves my area. . . .
>
> If I know my problem, I can likely solve it. If I don't know my problem, I might need some help finding it.[4]

The sort of problem we're out to find will lead to a superior solution for both sides, one that broadens the deal. While the process starts with prenegotiation value mapping, it culminates in discovery. At this point in the continuum, discovery is less about exploiting information and more about probing the other person's unmet—and often unspoken—needs for the greater good. Social psychologists call this "perspective-taking." Pink explains it this way:

> When confronted with an unusual or complex situation involving other people, how do we make sense of what's going on? Do we examine it from only our own point of view? Or do we have "the capability to step outside [our] own experience and imagine the emotions, perceptions, and motivations of another?"[5]

Perspective-taking is the opposite of posturing or manipulating or bloviating on why you're right and the other person is wrong. The operative verb is *asking*. Questions connect us—naturally, organically. They foster a collaborative mindset while expanding our knowledge base. No buyer comes in knowing all the details behind a product or service. No seller can be expected to guess the ins and outs of a buyer's organization. When we add some question marks to the ends of our sentences, a negotiation becomes an education.

The more clearly you discern the other side's point of view, no matter how confused it may seem, the firmer your handle on their needs. The more information you gather, the more accurate your targeting of tradeable assets. As you learn the other person's story, you can adjust your own accordingly. You might say something along the lines of, "Now that I understand your priorities, we have a pro software edition that's probably more suitable." (To be clear, this isn't just about upselling. You might decide that a *cheaper* edition would serve just as well, a great way to gain a buyer's trust.)

To sum up, you can't match your assets to someone else's needs if you don't know what they need. And you can't know what they need without asking thoughtful questions. In the following example, a commercial printer keeps at it until he finds a more creative deal.

Buyer: So as I was saying, your competition has come in and you're going to have to sharpen your pencil. I need you to come down at least 10 percent.

Seller: I want to work with you, but I can't just cut my price. And I certainly can't come down $25,000. I gave you a really good number right out of the chute.

Buyer: But you're still way high for us.

Seller: Okay, I hear you. Maybe there's something I could do to help you cut your costs and help me at the same time.

Buyer: You've got my attention. What do you have in mind?

Seller: Tell me this: What exactly do you do with these marketing pieces? Give them out at trade shows? Or do you use mass mailing?

Buyer: No, they're attached to our ads in trade journals. They're perforated inserts, so people can tear them out.

Seller: That's interesting. And how many trade journals do you advertise in?

Buyer: About a baker's dozen.

Seller: And are they all put together in the same area?

Buyer: No, they're assembled at twelve different locations, all across the country.

Seller: Right now we're shipping in bulk to your central Dallas warehouse. Then what do you do, reship them to the publishers?

Buyer: That's right.

Seller: And who pays the freight, you or them?

Buyer: We do.

Seller: Do you know what the freight costs you?

Buyer: Sure, I get the bill paid, and I can tell you it isn't cheap. Costs us nearly fifty grand.

Seller: That much? Any idea what kind of discount you get from your carriers?

Buyer: About 30 percent off their rack rate—we're not one of their big customers.

Seller: Thirty percent, that's all? Hmm, let me think. (*Long pause.*) Look, here's something that might help you out. Why don't we do the freight for you?

Buyer: How would that work?

Seller: We could send directly to all twelve sites on a prepay and add basis—we pay for the shipping and bill you later.

Buyer: I'm not sure I understand. What does that do for us?

Seller: Since we're a big national shipper, we'll get double your discount, which cuts your shipping bill in half. That saves you the $25,000 right there. Plus you're offloading the job of getting the pieces out. What do you think?

Buyer: Wow, that sounds good to me.

Seller: Here's what I'd like to ask you in return. If you can pay us net thirty instead of net sixty, I think I can sell this to my boss. Could that work on your end?

Buyer: Let me take it upstairs to accounting, but I think we may have a deal.

Who's the winner here? If the buyer's objective was to save $25,000, the new shipping arrangement does the trick. If the seller's goal was to stand by her quoted price, she's a big winner as well. Instead of making quick concessions, the two sides stood their ground and wrestled out the problem. Their reward? An agreement that is better for both.

R-E-S-P-E-C-T

Where bargaining contains an element of performance (if not theatrics), creative dealmaking demands a sincere interest in the other party, in their desires and concerns. It's a whole other mindset, a new way of engaging others and considering what they have to say. To move people, we need to treat them as humans, not econs. We must speak to their emotions. Helping them *feel* better about the deal may outweigh a clinical analysis of a tradeoff's benefits. In addition to informational questions, one especially persuasive tool is advice-seeking. Beyond learning something useful, as Adam Grant points out, you'll be showing respect and "encouraging others to take our perspectives."[6] In an experiment where people negotiated a commercial property sale, Grant noted:

> When the sellers focused on their goal of getting the highest possible price, only 8 percent reached a successful agreement. When the sellers asked the buyers for advice on how to meet their goals, 42 percent reached a successful agreement. Asking for advice encouraged greater cooperation and information sharing. . . .
>
> When we ask people for advice, we [show] that we respect and admire their insights and expertise. Since most people are matchers, they tend to respond favorably and feel motivated to support us in return.[7]

Once you begin to see people as *people*—as three-dimensional subjects, not objects to manipulate or opponents to overcome—you'll gain a broader view of the negotiation. As you extract the other side's story, it will soon be apparent that you're not the only one under pressure. As a result, you'll feel less heat to make hasty concessions. You'll have more patience to bring your assets to light and have them fully valued. By giving both parties time to develop their stories, you'll find options that might have escaped a cursory glance.

While the discovery process is more cooperative in creative dealmaking, it retains a competitive element. But instead of an adversarial joust to gain the larger concessions, it's a duel of competing narratives, a conflict of perspectives in pursuit of a creative outcome. (Think: Lennon and McCartney.) After all, it's in both sides' interest for the most efficient, productive, and profitable solution to emerge, no matter who thought of it first.

As part of your anchoring strategy, you might agree to an informal ground rule at the outset: Both sides will do their best to stay open-minded, not dismissing the other's ideas out of hand. Instead of shooting down your proposal in defense of my own, I'll tame my ego and welcome the debate. I'll ask myself, *What can I learn here?* And I'll say to you, "I'm not sure that will work, but can you tell me more about it?"

After hashing things out, we still may have different ideas about what's fair—and that's more than okay. It's the grist for creative conflict and a better-for-both outcome. On top of any tangible returns, two-sided discovery generates some very valuable intangibles: improved communication, greater transparency, tighter alignment, deeper understanding . . . and the potential for even more opportunities, in the current deal and down the road.

It's Not Just the Money

I'll never forget the seminar participant who introduced herself to us as "the world's worst negotiator."

"That's quite a claim," I said. "What happened?"

"I saw this house I really liked, and it was listed at $500,000," she said. "So I decided to make a really low offer: $400,000. And you know what the broker said?"

"Tell me."

"'Great, you've got yourself a deal!' Wasn't that dumb of me?"

Thinking she might live in a place where real estate values were underwater, I asked, "What's the market like in your neighborhood?"

She said, "Oh, the market's been great! I bought a couple years ago, and the house is worth about $600,000 now."

And I asked myself: How could someone be disappointed after getting a 20 percent discount on an asset that appreciates 50 percent in two years? Didn't she get a great value?

The answer is yes . . . and no. Objectively, we could say the woman snared an outstanding value. *Subjectively*, however, she felt shortchanged—but why? Hypothetically, suppose the seller's agent had flinched at her initial bid: "Wow, just $400,000? I'm obligated by the state to take any good-faith offer back to the owners, but that's way under market. Look, let me check in with them and see how they react—you never know."

A day later, the broker calls the woman back and says, "I can't believe it! You know what the owners said? If you'll agree today, they'll sell to you for $410,000. I was surprised, to tell you the truth, but they're going through a divorce and are ready to close. Congratulations!"

Had events played out that way, I can guarantee you that the buyer would have been happier paying ten thousand dollars *more* than she did in real life. Talk to any salesperson, and they'll tell you the same thing. They have customers who get their best price but are always grumbling and nibbling for extras. And they have others paying top dollar who are happy as larks.

How can that be? In any negotiation, satisfaction with a deal corresponds with the *subjective* value of the outcome. The more work it takes for someone to earn a concession, the more value it conveys—and the more satisfied they are to get it.

In a one-off bargaining scenario, the other party's contentment may seem of little import. But once we advance to creative dealmaking, with the prospect of an ongoing relationship, every negotiation affects the next round. A satisfied counterpart is money in the bank—*your* bank.

- When the other side feels they've done a good job of negotiating, they're apt to be less suspicious and more trusting the next time around. That's a key factor in arriving at better-for-both agreements.

- When you make concessions slowly, incrementally, and even a little grudgingly, you lower the other side's expectations in future deals and for outstanding issues in the current one. Our research shows that expectations are inversely correlated to satisfaction—the lower the first, the higher the second. (It's here that concession-making overlaps with target-setting.)

- Conversely, if you're a buyer and you up your offer 15 percent off the bat to meet the seller's price, it's a safe bet that they'll build in an 18 or 20 percent margin the next time.

- When the ZOPA looks narrow and you have little objective room to move, it's important to eke maximum subjective value out of any concession—even when it's something you could offer without pain. Instead of saying, "Sure, that's no problem," you'll do better with, "Gee, I don't know, I'll have to think that over." Or, "I'd like to do that for you, but it's not really for me to decide. Let me take it to the executive team and see what I can work out." A day later you say, "Look, they owed me a favor, so we're going to give you that." Say *no* before you say *yes*, even when you know that's where you're heading. Trust us: Their appreciation will soar.

Other Dealmaking Tactics

In bargaining, *priming* is a form of anchoring, a subtle technique to influence the other side's expectations. In dealmaking, priming sets expectations *for the negotiation itself.* It makes a two-sided exploration more thoroughgoing and creative. A seller might say to a buyer, "Helena, I've got your RFP and I think I understand what you want, and you've got my proposal, but I'd like to spend some time going over it. I want to make sure that what I have in mind matches what you really need. I'm going to have lots of questions for you, and I hope you'll have plenty for me—let's allow an hour for that phone call." The seller is signaling both an interest in moving beyond price and a seriousness of purpose.

In *wooing*, we make clear how much we value the other party, regardless of any differences. The buyer might tell the seller, "Ryan, I know we're not that close right now, but I have to believe there's a way to work this out. I think you're a great fit for us, and we'd really like to do business with your organization. Let's keep talking." By expressing our desire to reach agreement, and intimating that more deals might lay down the road, we'll encourage the other side to keep slogging along with us through a rough patch.

Build momentum. As any hostage negotiator can attest, you can put the other person at ease by deferring more difficult issues. Reach first for the lower-hanging fruit. By racking up some easy agreements and reassuring the other party that your differences are bridgeable, you'll create positive momentum for the tougher stuff later on. As people make progress early on in a negotiation, they grow more committed to seeing it through. An early "yes" or two on secondary points may soften the other side's stance on bigger ones.

Stick to your guns. It's one thing to be prepared to compromise to reach a more comprehensive agreement. It's another to abandon your position without waging an honest struggle. By standing behind your viewpoint until you and your counterpart find something better, you're doing your bit for creative conflict. Remember, it's friction that forces both parties to look at the deal in a new way. *A corollary tactic*: The broken record, where you simply repeat your arguments instead of feeling compelled to soften them. As ex-Google executive Jonathan Rosenberg reminds us, "Repetition doesn't spoil the prayer."[8]

Establish limits for the other party. There's a difference between what people say they want in a negotiation and what they actually need to bring back to their stakeholders. When it comes to stipulations, there are two baskets: "must-haves" and "would-like-to-haves." Don't take people's demands at face value. It's on you to push back where appropriate. If they believe they can get what they want without real reciprocation, why would they bother racking their brains for more creative tradeoffs?

Our public seminars draw a diverse and colorful crowd. At one event in Los Angeles, a top marriage broker revealed to us the secret to her success: "When people come to see me, they tell me what they want. I talk to them and find out what they need. Then, after I give them what they need, they forget what they want."

Insist on a quid pro quo (until you don't). Bargaining tends to be constrained by firm either/or positions. Creative dealmaking, by contrast, looks for novel ways to serve mutual interests:

- YES, I can give that, BUT here's what I'd need in return . . .

- NO, I can't give that, BUT here's what I can offer instead . . .

- IF I do that for you, THEN I'll need this in exchange . . .

Reciprocation is the beating heart of creative dealmaking. Requesting a quid pro quo is always in order, especially when the other side hits you up for an eleventh-hour nibble or escalation. If there's no practical tradeoff and you choose to cede the concession, it should be understood that the other side owes you one in the next round.

With *charm and disarm,* one side proposes an agreement in principle. The French are masters of this tactic: "Don't worry, we'll hammer out the minor details later." In bargaining, charm and disarm can be a deceptively devastating power move, leaving the other party overcommitted to a deal that isn't nearly as closed as they'd thought. In creative dealmaking, it can sometimes be useful as a temporary workaround when you're stalled over a sticking point. But beware: By soft-pedaling conflict, a premature commitment can create the illusion that you have no real differences. When the conflict inevitably reemerges, it may be even harder to negotiate a better-for-both solution.

The considered response. Also known as the pregnant pause, the considered response is a variation of the reflective response, a great way to slow yourself down. It preserves creative tension and allows better ideas to bubble to the surface. As an ancillary benefit, it lends more weight to whatever you say next, even if it's only to postpone a decision. The considered response has a long and honored history in Japan, as Howard Van Zandt explained in a classic piece in *Harvard Business Review*:

> Americans often don't know how to cope with silence. They can't understand what is going on. Briefly, this is what is happening:
>
> When a pause or impasse in the discussions develops, the Japanese remain quiet, not feeling a compulsion to say anything. . . . When a couple of minutes have passed, and no comment is forthcoming, Americans become uneasy and feel that they must make some sort of statement. It is at this point that they often voluntarily give in on a disputed point or say something they should not say, just to get the conversation going again.[9]

The power of uncertainty. A first cousin to the considered response is the *power of uncertainty,* where you leave the other side off-balance by saying, "I haven't formed an opinion on that," or simply, "I don't know." There's no shame in being less than omniscient. By buying time to caucus or simply to think, you've kept your options open. In creative dealmaking, that's just where you want to be.

Summary

- Once bargaining hits a wall, creative dealmaking can lead to a better-for-both solution by matching one side's assets with the other's needs.

- The primary strategy in this mode is *value mapping,* which surfaces subtle, hidden assets and reveals mutual gain tradeoffs.

- As more information is shared in discovery, both sides gain insights into the other's needs—and how to craft a value proposition that can meet them.

- Ask questions, and lots of them. It's the best way to expand our knowledge base and to collaboratively find the problem that needs to be solved.

- Even when you fully intend to give something up, do it slowly and reluctantly. By making the other party work for the concession, you'll increase its subjective value. You'll also incentivize them to generate more profitable solutions.

- What the other side *wants* is not the same as what they *need*. Set limits on the first while doing all you can to satisfy the second.

- The quid pro quo is the essence of creative dealmaking. Before making a no-strings-attached concession, consider how the other side might be able to reciprocate. By enriching the creative process, quid pro quos add value to the outcome.

Part Four

THE PARTNER

(RELATIONSHIP BUILDING)

Self-contained projects   Strategic partnerships

10

Joining Forces

The call came on a late Friday afternoon, the kind of news every purchaser dreads. Days before his back-to-school inventory was slated to arrive, Brad Young, Staples' vice president of global manufacturing and sourcing, heard from one of his key vendors.

"Listen, Brad, I'm really sorry, but we had an explosion in our main plant this morning. Thank God no one was hurt, but it's a major mechanical failure, and production is shut tight. We won't be up and running again for two months. We can't fill your order—the whole season is shot."

In the office supply business, three-ring binders are a core strategic product. They bring customers into stores. Though Staples had multisourced the item, the downed plant accounted for 25 percent of the chain's inventory. As we retold the story in *Supply Chain Management Review*, Brad was staring at disaster.[1] How could he compensate with next to no time left on the clock?

Brad phoned his most reliable supplier in the category, the owner of a small paper goods factory in a faraway land—let's call it Egypt. It was midnight, Cairo time, and he knew he'd woken the man up. "Listen, Rahman, a thousand apologies, but I'm in a bind." He explained the emergency, praying that Rahman could deliver at least a chunk of his shortfall. Brad had done the math in his head. He was prepared to pay a 30 percent premium for rush production. He just hoped it wouldn't go higher than that.

And Rahman said, "Okay, tomorrow's a holiday for us, but I'll start up my plant to run three shifts and get you all the extra volume by the end of next week. And we'll keep the price the same. You can get me a purchase order Monday. Brad, I know how hard you work. Don't worry about it, I've got you covered. Enjoy your weekend."

What do we make of this? Brad won some huge concessions without so much as asking for them. Again, negotiating is the act of bridging a gap to make an agreement. But here the two sides had no apparent gap—ergo, no negotiation, right?

In fact, the agreement was the fruit of *eight years* of negotiating across the entire continuum. The first time they did business, when Brad's focus was to keep Staples competitive in the binder market, he bargained Rahman down to his bottom line. After a time, the supplier told him, "I want to keep working with you, but I'm making almost nothing on our deal." Brad, a production manager in a former life, flew fifteen hours from Boston to Cairo to conduct a plant tour. He shared ideas to lower costs and raise efficiency that helped keep Rahman afloat. Two years later, Brad advised the vendor to expand into higher-margin product lines, adding some volume orders to get them out of the starting gate. In an exemplary demonstration of creative dealmaking, he challenged Rahman to get better while providing how-to help as needed. Rahman prospered; his revenues tripled. Brick by brick, the two sides built a genuine rapport.

By the time of the binder crisis, Brad had invested years of purposeful development into the Egyptian firm. You could say that he'd *anchored* Rahman to the idea that a long-term partnership was to their mutual benefit. With a standing relationship based on assistance and support, Brad felt comfortable in reaching out and sharing his vulnerability. Rahman was motivated to solve Staples' problem without exploiting it for extra profit. He jumped at the opportunity to reciprocate. The relationship itself added value to the deal.

A Mode for This Moment

The third and final piece of the continuum, relationship building, is the most multifaceted of the three. Among larger companies—

Apple and Nike, Toyota and Subaru, Toyota and Uber—it's the mode of the moment in the "new world-class, knowledge-worker-based, global economy."[2] In the current era, as sellers' titles have changed from "sales manager" to "account manager" to "relationship manager," basic bargaining techniques—or even quid pro quo matching—are no longer sufficient. Even in smaller companies, salespeople spend half or more of their time fixing problems for existing customers—in maintaining relationships. In the face of extreme volatility and withering market pressures, strategic allies are more vital than ever.

The hallmarks of these negotiations are complexity and repetition. One-time transactions don't qualify. The mode's subcontinuum ranges from temporary affiliations and discrete contracts to longer-term agreements, interwoven supply chains, and interlocking directorates. The apex business-to-business relationship, a *strategic alliance,* is positively symbiotic. Each side negotiates for their partner's interests as much as for their own. At the same time, they stay on the lookout to expand their joint ventures. As we've seen, United and Starbucks had a good thing going from their first creative deal. But when it came time to renew their coffee supply and cooperative marketing agreement for a fourth three-year term, they broadened the partnership into music. In a pilot run, United presented an in-flight entertainment program based on Starbucks-produced recordings of late-career Ray Charles.

As we move from single issues to multiple considerations, from shared suspicion to interdependence, we need a radically different set of strategies and skills. Most of all, relationship building calls for a new mental model. In building a true partnership, tit-for-tat reciprocation is counterproductive. Withholding information can throw an operation into disarray. Transparency and fair play are paramount.

Though competition remains part of the equation, it takes a different form. Two-sided creative conflict strengthens the relationship, grows the profit pie, and shows the way to future opportunities. The two parties advance from total cost of ownership (TCO) and total business opportunities (TBO) to *total value optimization* (TVO), where they match assets and needs for maximum gains over the long haul. Instead of extracting or exchanging value, strategic allies compete to do good turns for one another and generate shared profits. The more persuasive you are in winning the other side to your viewpoint, the stronger the relationship will be.

As in any good marriage, a fair and satisfying outcome isn't always a 50-50 split of the TVO gains. Depending on the situation, one side or the other may take one for the team. When a supplier caters to a regular customer by developing a new solution, they're probably making the larger initial outlay and assuming the greater risk. While the mutual benefits may be undeniable, there's no one right way to share them. The buyer may say, "Whatever you come up with, you can have all the savings for the first year, and then we'll take 60 percent going forward." Sometimes one side is in trouble and needs a "gotcha": *I'll bite the bullet and give it to you this time, and I know you'll make it up to me next time.* At other times, it may be in my long-term interest to make you feel like you won the transaction. Or I'll throw in an anti-nibble: *No, that's too much, I can't take that.* The relationship's future outweighs who gets the odd extra percentage point in any one deal.

At times, however, even the closest partners square off. Deals *never* proceed precisely according to plan—there are always unforeseen events. The more complex the agreement, the more vulnerable it is to misinterpretation. In confronting their differences, the two sides may revert to quid pro quo matching and even some price haggling. But even when they veer back to the left on the continuum, their tactics will be softer. (Vehement trash talking, for example, is a bell you can't unring.) Profits still count, of course, but the priority is the alliance and the synergies it brings.

In general, our goals in this mode are qualitative as well as quantitative. We're aiming for a quicker response to problems, higher morale, and, most important, an enhanced ability to find those juicy tradeoffs and a superior payoff. Once a project is underway, all sorts of new value opportunities emerge. As each side gains more insight into the other's capabilities and needs, work can be adjusted midflight. Creative dealmakers learn to trust one another, within limits; strategic partners are *confident* the other side will come through. As we saw with Brad and Rahman, alliances are built through negotiation and consolidated by performance—and a shared investment in the future. A sort of two-sided leverage is embedded within the relationship. As the political scientist Robert Axelrod wrote in *The Evolution of Cooperation*:

> Diamond markets, for example, are famous for the way their members exchange millions of dollars' worth of goods with only a verbal pledge and a handshake. The key factor is that the participants know they will be dealing with each other again and again. Therefore any attempt to exploit the situation will simply not pay. . . . The foundation of cooperation is . . . the durability of the relationship.[3]

As a supplier builds a special relationship and compiles a solid track record, the ripple effects are transformational:

> The consistent production of results not only causes customers to increase their reorders, it also compels them to consistently recommend you to others. Thus, your customers become your key sales and marketing people.[4]

A caveat: Not all business deals are destined to usher in long-term relationships. Before jumping into a partnership, organizations need to ask themselves: Has the other party consistently met their obligations—or, better yet, exceeded them? If so, it may be time to talk about going steady.

Co-Opetition

When opportunity knocks, the fiercest rivals may carve out a space where they join forces for their mutual good. Apple and Google, two of the four largest companies in the world, go head-to-head in a myriad of critical marketing battlegrounds: web browsers, smartphone operating systems and hardware, PC-operating software, voice-activated assistants (Siri vs. "Hey Google"), app stores (iTunes vs. Google Play), digital rights management (Apple TV vs. YouTube). But since 2007, the two tech behemoths have worked hand-in-glove in one extremely lucrative arena. In exchange for a healthy royalty check (up to $12 billion a year), Apple has made Google their default search engine across their devices, most notably on the iPhone. As Bruce Sewell, Apple's former general counsel, told the *New York Times*, "We have this sort of strange term in Silicon Valley: co-opetition. . . . You have brutal competition, but at the same time, you have necessary cooperation."[5]

It's a spectacular example of revenue-sharing symbiosis. When an iPhone user goes to Apple browser Safari and asks Apple assistant Siri to find a Thai restaurant nearby, Siri uses Google Search to find a place around the block that just happens to be a Google advertiser. Google reaps the ad revenue and kicks a share of it back to Apple. While this exclusive arrangement may be challenged by federal antitrust action, neither principal will let go of it voluntarily. Apple can't afford to ditch Google because no other search company could pay them nearly that much. Google can't afford to leave Apple because so much search originates on iPhones.

Co-opetition can be found in any number of sectors. For example:

- Verizon, AT&T, and T-Mobile routinely make deals to add capacity on the other organization's networks.

- Chemical companies will compete ruthlessly in one product space while sourcing particular chemicals from one another.

- When one oil producer has a valuable lease and another the requisite pipelines and field equipment in the vicinity, they'll engage in farm-in or farm-out joint ventures.

In all of these situations, it takes a creative approach—in the face of overt conflict—to work out a deal to benefit both sides. It also demands a two-sided mindset. As we've noted, the added value still needs to be distributed. Collaboration has its limits. As Apple's Sewell observed, "You have to be able to maintain those relationships and not burn a bridge. . . . At the same time, when you're negotiating on behalf of your company and you're trying to get the best deal, then, you know, the gloves come off."[6]

One more point: Apple constructed the deal to be renegotiated at regular intervals. This gave them the ability to make sure that the contract they'd signed was the one they were getting—that Google was living up to its side of the agreement. As the companies' complex relationship changes, and the world changes around them, the arrangement can be adjusted accordingly.

Positive Leverage

Leverage building contains its own continuum. In bargaining, and especially in one-time or highly charged transactions, *consequential leverage* bluntly reminds the counterparty why they need you. A buyer may point out how important they are to a supplier's business, laying out their options—the consequences—if expectations go unmet. In creative dealmaking, as we saw in the last chapter, leverage is the stuff of quid pro quos. What I do for you ties explicitly to what you are doing for me.

But in a long-term agreement, in the context of a giving relationship, leverage takes on a very different character. It becomes *positive leverage*, extra help with no strings attached. When someone offers an unsolicited "delight factor," they gain nothing tangible; often they're inconveniencing themselves. But they're also banking goodwill, the hard currency of strategic alliances. The value of the relationship trumps the transaction's bottom line.

There is very little downside to positive leverage—as long as the other side meets two criteria. The first speaks to character. It's not enough for the other side to be honest—they need to be *intrepid*. You can count on them in adversity. Delight factors backfire with opportunists.

The second requirement is an ongoing interaction that appears to have a future. It's usually a mistake to lavish favors on someone with whom you have little experience. (They may simply pocket the goodies and expect more the next time.) Likewise, it makes no business sense to go too many extra miles in what may be a one-and-done deal.

When the other side is doing the leveraging, of course, you may not have a choice. Frank Mobus told a story about a three-year construction project in Barstow, California, in the heart of the Mojave Desert, for a new cluster of outlet malls. Frank's paving company received bids from two asphalt suppliers and chose the lower one. Two months in, the subcontractor sent him a registered letter: "Dear Frank, your people ran into some delays last week and it looked like the job was going to go on penalty"—at a cost to Frank's company of $5,000 a day. "So your foreman asked us if we'd keep our plant running all night for three nights so they could pave around the clock. We were happy to help you out." Attached was an invoice: "70 hours of overtime, no charge per Steve."

A few weeks later, Frank received another letter. This one referenced a broken Barber Green, the jumbo-sized paver: "Your crew was sitting there, waiting for someone to come in from San Bernardino to repair it, so we sent over our machine so you wouldn't waste the day." And the invoice: "Barber Green rate, $1,500/hour, no charge per Steve."

At the end of year one, after half a dozen similar letters, the rival asphalt supplier came back and offered Frank a better price—substantially lower, in fact, than Steve's rate. Frank called Steve in and told him, "Look, you're really going to have to do something about your price."

And Steve said, "Wait a second, Frank, do you remember all the things we've done for you?" He pulled out copies of the registered letters and went through them, chapter and verse. "Now tell me honestly, Frank, do you get that service from every asphalt plant?"

No, they didn't, Frank had to admit.

"Do we give you exceptional service?"

Yes, you do, Frank said.

"Is that worth a premium?"

And Frank acknowledged that it was. Though he renegotiated the second year of his deal with Steve, he still spent more than he would have paid the rival. Steve had weaponized his positive leverage, turning favors into chits and calling them in. His delight factors were actually a form of *nibbling*, with reverse English. Though he was giving, not taking or reneging (the traditional nibble), the objective was the same. Steve leveraged his thoughtful generosity to put Frank on his back foot.

HOW TO BE A GOOD PARTNER

How are positive long-term alliances sustained? It goes back to what our parents taught us early in life:

- Play nice with others.

- Share your toys.

- Don't always take the biggest piece of pie.

- Take turns.

- Keep your promises.

In bargaining, our mindset is "I've got mine." In relationship building, it becomes "I've got your back."

RELATIONSHIP BUILDING TACTICS

Though relationship building is mostly strategic in nature, tactics also come into play. In the spirit of transparency and good faith, these tactics are very different from the ones we use in bargaining.

Bargaining	Relationship building
Flinch	Reassure
Trash Talking	Straight Talking
Leave Room	Realistic Offer
Be Stingy	Be Generous
Walk Out	Stay Engaged
Take It or Leave It	Work It Out
Tactical Deadline	Offer More Time
Charm & Disarm	Genuine Compromise
Nibbling	Delight Factors
Escalation	Exceed Commitments
Keeping Score	Helping Out

The Value of Trust

The late, great Oliver Williamson, the Nobel Prize–winning Berkeley economist, is best known for his work on transaction cost economics. Williamson distinguished between isolated purchases of standardized commodities, on the one hand, and repeated deals for more customized items, on the other—the deals that give rise to relationships. Transaction costs consist of three main elements:

- **Search and information**, the expense of finding the best value on the market

- **Bargaining and decision making**, the cost of the negotiation process, including legal overhead

- **Policing and enforcement**, to make sure the deal you get is the one you agreed to—and to spell out your recourse when it isn't[7]

When doubt reigns, everything gets more expensive. Contracts get overgrown, with both sides on guard against ambiguities and loopholes. Lawyers inject one-sided language on terms and conditions—a prelude to extra rounds of negotiation (both external and internal) and fine-toothed redlining. Disagreements unresolved at the table get kicked up the chain of command, which means even more delay and expense.

The stronger the relationship, the more transaction costs can be pared to add value. When we're less worried about the other side's opportunism, contracts can be less intricate. Legal vetting is less aggressive. Organizations with outsourcing relationships "based upon mutual trust," rather than penalties, enjoy "a 'trust dividend' worth as much as 40 percent of the total value of the contract."[8]

Warren Buffett's Berkshire Hathaway was a major stockholder in Walmart for many years. The two companies' top executives had longstanding ties. When Walmart sold Buffett a wholesaler subsidiary, the Oracle of Omaha "had a single meeting of about two hours with Tom Schoewe, Wal-Mart's CFO, and we then shook hands," according to Buffett's famous annual shareholder letter. "Twenty-nine days later Wal-Mart had its money. We did no 'due diligence.' We knew everything would be exactly as Wal-Mart said it would be—and it was."[9] The value of the handshake deal? A mere $1.5 billion.

We know a construction company that chose a favored contractor for a complex project worth more than $750 million. Thanks to their durable relationship and deep reservoir of mutual confidence, the contract was two pages long.

"Otherish" Giving

When businesspeople in the Far East sit down to negotiate, they may begin with an exchange of gifts, followed by tea, an elaborate tray of sweets, and gracious small talk. The Japanese are legendary for hosting elaborate meals and endless toasts before getting down to brass tacks. These preliminaries work wonders in reducing tension and getting talks off to a constructive start. But they're less familiar in the United States, where people are trained to get down to business and cut to the chase. In terms of relationship building, that's a missed opportunity. Rapport can make or break a budding partnership, especially when it comes to the care and feeding of long-term agreements. A positive climate inspires free-wheeling, value-enhancing discussion. It promotes critical candor. It helps strategic allies make it through trying times.

While pricey gifts may be culturally inappropriate in New York or Los Angeles, there's nothing to stop you from sharing a tip about that new Italian restaurant, or from showing an interest in the other party's children or hobbies or alma mater. As you ease into the negotiation, and disagreement rears its head, it's even more important to treat your counterpart as a collaborator, not an antagonist. We can disagree without being disagreeable or dismissing the other side's ideas off the cuff. Creative dealmaking tactics—avoiding the "hard no," charm-and-disarm, the reflective response—are helpful in relationship building as well.

While the art of giving predominates in this mode, it's not indiscriminate. One practical tack is to modify your reciprocation strategy—to move from "negotiated giving" (a form of matching) to what Adam Grant calls "otherish giving" or "generous tit for tat." When allies have yet to fully prove themselves, it's well-advised to stay vigilant as you set a benevolent tone:

> Where selfless givers make the mistake of trusting others all the time, otherish givers start out with trust as the default assumption, but they're willing to adjust their reciprocity styles in exchanges with someone who appears to be a taker by action or reputation . . . taking care to trust but verify. . . .
>
> By looking for opportunities to benefit others and themselves, otherish givers are able to think in more complex ways. . . . Instead of just giving away value like selfless givers, otherish givers create value first. By the time they give slices of pie away, the entire pie is big enough that there's plenty left to claim for themselves: they can give more *and* take more.[10]

In a Dutch meta-analysis of twenty-eight studies, Grant reports, otherish givers were consistently the most effective negotiators.

Forewarning

There's a classic negotiating story involving the rock band Van Halen. The group's standard contract included a rider for particular drinks and food items to be catered backstage for the musicians. Under the category of "munchies," after potato chips and nuts and pretzels, the rider stipulated M&Ms, with an all-caps proviso: "WARNING: ABSOLUTELY NO BROWN ONES." A failure to follow this mandate to the letter meant the concert promoter would forfeit the show, a financial disaster. On the surface, the M&M rider seemed outrageous, a bizarre self-indulgence for lead singer David Lee Roth. But there was a method to Van Halen's madness. They traveled with state-of-the-art stage equipment, including an enormous lighting rig. It took eighteen trucks to haul it all from place to place. To make sure their shows went off without a hitch, the band needed to know that the promoter had thoroughly read the contract, most of all its technical requirements. The M&Ms were a litmus test, a mechanism to assure that the band would get the deal they'd signed for.

Holding the other party to account is especially critical in long-term agreements (LTAs), where two organizations may be joined at the hip for years. There are two ways an LTA goes south. One is too *much* conflict, an overreliance on caveman bargaining tactics. But the other extreme is more common—and more dangerous. It goes back to Deming's notion of negotiation sans conflict, the idea that good faith is all we need to steer clear of differences. In established relationships, there's a gravitational pull to get along by going along. But don't forget: You're being paid to stand up for your firm's interests, not to defer to the other side. That confusion has destroyed many a promising alliance.

One problem with LTAs is that they generally start out so well. At the outset of a relationship, people are reluctant to say, "That sounds good now, but let's think about what might go wrong later." Open disagreement feels like bad manners. It's a big mistake, however, to assume that conflict is dead and buried once a contract is signed. In reality, the negotiation has just begun. No matter how friendly the process, no matter how sincere the two sides' mutual esteem, they must still find an evenhanded way to divvy up their winnings. Moving forward, they'll still need to perform as agreed upon. None of that happens automatically. It requires constant vigilance.

In bargaining, negotiators often nibble for last-minute concessions. In deals between strategic partners, a similar tactic can be even more insidious. When faced with some dire need, one side or the other may fall into nibbling *on the agreement.* They begin slipping on commitments. Vendors pad their margins, miss deadlines, overrun costs. Customers delay payment or ask for extras outside the scope of the deal. Joint innovation projects lose steam and slide into the realm of the half-hearted. This nibbling often isn't deliberate; it may even be unconscious. When you're dealing with a global merchandising director or some other higher-up, they're apt to be spread too thin to give you the attention you're counting on.

Benign neglect is still neglect, however. Left unchallenged, lower performance standards become the new normal. The relationship is corrupted. The LTA spirals downward until management gets fed up and tells purchasing to throw the bums out—or, at minimum, to broaden the supply base and hedge the company's bets. Either way, the advantages of a special relationship with a dedicated vendor are lost.

Power isn't static. In most buy-sell scenarios in a competitive marketplace, the buyer has more leverage early on. Over time, however, power tends to shift to the seller. When a longtime supplier gets complacent, it's up to the buyer to flag the problem. That's an uncomfortable conversation—nobody wants to be the skunk at the garden party. To express disagreements with a valued ally, you need to move from back foot to front, which demands a lot of energy. It's so much easier to hope for the best. But shying away from conflict—or stewing silently—won't make the issue go away. Unexpressed grievances corrode an alliance from within. At some point, the tension congeals into cynicism or erupts into a blame game of angry ultimatums.

How can we do better? The short answer: open communication. We advise our clients to explicitly *forewarn* the other side, to anticipate differences and have the freedom to raise them. You don't need M&Ms—a frank conversation will do. Choose a receptive moment, perhaps in the afterglow of closing. Pause from the celebration to say something like, "I know both of us have the best of intentions for this deal. But I also know there's bound to be some headaches as we work together. If you see something wrong, I want you to know you can come to me any time—and please don't wait and let it fester. And I hope I'll be able to do the same with you."

The ideal is for *both* parties to stay on their front foot, to balance cooperation and competition—to live on the edge of the inside. Creative conflict preserves a healthy equilibrium, where both sides keep getting their fair share. Quality relationships are strengthened by dealing proactively with differences, not pretending they don't exist. In our experience, negotiators perceived as honest advocates are more highly regarded than passive accommodationists.

To follow through, you'll need concrete ground rules for monitoring disputes. You'll need ways to track the alliance and make sure it's still achieving its original purpose—or to consider whether the purpose has changed. Both sides must be ready to answer questions like these:

- Can we rely on each other to share bad news as well as good news in a timely fashion?

- What will we do when something goes wrong?

- How will we negotiate changes?

- How can we improve our communication to avoid repeating the same problem?

The best marriages, according to the psychotherapist Daphne de Marneffe, "involve people who can deal with strong negative emotions—and who are clear-eyed about how hard it can be. They don't avoid anger, but they don't indulge it. They tackle hard issues without shutting down. They apologize for their own bad behavior."[11]

The same applies to matrimony in business. With a proactive framework in place, you'll be able to weather rough patches and get the project back on track. Handled well, the airing of differences can strengthen a relationship. It surfaces important issues that would otherwise remain hidden. Though relationship building is by nature a cooperative pursuit, it is our differences—as always—that drive the creative process.

Don't Fall in Love

Deals in this mode are tricky because our social norms come back into play. But while kinder, gentler behavior is expected between allies, we can't forget that we're still in the market—and that no alliance lasts forever. In business, tomorrow is never precisely like today. People get fired, hired, and promoted; the external environment is perpetually in flux. No matter how committed we may be to sharing and caring, the relationship will prosper only as long as it helps both sides.

The pitfalls in relationship building are most dangerous when one partner is significantly more powerful than the other. One of our clients, an automotive parts manufacturer, had a highly lucrative arrangement with GM that brought in more than half their revenues. After ten years of business together, they went to bid on a new contract—and were stunned to hear, "Before we consider your bid, we want you to pay us up front for the cost savings you made on your last program." Pay to play! GM figured our client would have no choice but to sell at a bargain basement price, if only to keep their plant running. They were over a barrel.

We asked about their other customers. "Well," they said, "we do a little business with Honda."

"And how is that relationship?"

And they said, "Boy, it took us years to get their business. They sent their engineers to our plant and made us go to them to see how our parts were used. And after we got the first deal, it was more of the same—they were really demanding. But you know what, they really helped us improve our quality. And they always say it's important for us to make a fair profit."

And we said, "You need more customers like Honda."

The moral of the story? Don't fall in love with a business partner that keeps leaving you with the short end of the stick. It's easy to get stuck in an abusive relationship out of inertia or convenience or terror of the unknown. But beware. You don't want to wind up on *Dr. Phil* with the audience chanting, "Dump him, dump him!" Nor does it pay to become the exploitive party. At some point your partner will do one of two things: get even or get out. In a successful LTA, each party looks out for *both* sides' interests. That's the road to building mutual value.

Summary

- Relationship building is the preferred mode for any negotiation involving repetition and complexity. The apex relationship, with the most potential for expanding the value pie, is a long-term strategic alliance.

- At this point in the continuum, you're negotiating for the other side's interests as well as for your own.

- While cooperation is primary, the two parties still compete in pursuit of *total value optimization*, where assets and needs are matched for maximum benefits over time.

- A fair outcome isn't always an even split. The relationship's future outweighs the short-term bottom line.

- Positive leverage, typically in the form of delight factors, is appropriate in any long-term relationship where you can rely on the other side.

- Otherish givers trust their partners and set a generous tone, but remain watchful for backsliding.

- Don't fall in love. No business relationship lasts forever. When an alliance no longer works for both parties, it's time to find the door.

11

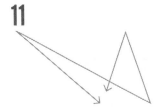

The Sole Source

Jerry Seinfeld: Congratulations, looks like things are going great with your new girlfriend.

George Costanza: No, they're not going great. The problem is I got no power in this relationship. Why should she have the upper hand? Just once I'd like the upper hand. I got no hand. No hand at all! How do I get the hand?

As the US economy gears more and more to customized solutions, sole-source relationships are a growing trend—and a compelling value proposition. By cultivating a sole source, buyers can harvest a wealth of creative tradeoffs and transaction cost advantages. Think of the overhead that might be trimmed by keeping an incumbent supplier instead of screening multiple responses to an RFP. Or how many hours an inhouse lawyer could save by redlining one umbrella contract instead of a raft of compartmentalized ones.

Sole sourcing is a boon for suppliers as well. Freed from dog-eat-dog competitive bidding, they can focus on meeting the purchaser's needs—on getting the job done *right*, without feeling pressed to cut corners. Over time, as buyer and seller build trust, they minimize the need for ground-up vetting or pages of contractual fine print.

When jobs are multisourced and Balkanized, accountability suffers. If one vendor is used for hardware, a second for software, a third for installation and maintenance, and a fourth for training, mistakes are fodder for finger-pointing. Worse yet, the vendors' advice may be unreliable. A maintenance company won't be eager to advise a client to replace a glitchy piece of hardware with a trouble-free alternative. A hardware firm will push its latest-and-greatest component over a simple software fix. When you're a hammer, as the saying goes, everything looks like a nail.

With preferred suppliers, on the other hand, there's nowhere to pass the buck. When a problem arises, it falls on the exclusive source to find an integrated, cost-effective solution. Over time, assuming a healthy seller-buyer dynamic, healthy habits are institutionalized. The two sides grow accustomed to joining together to create added value.

Yet despite their clear virtues, sole-source relationships are double-edged. For negotiators on the sourcing side, in particular, they are packed with landmines. Here is why: *When a sole source is relied upon for a product or service, power naturally moves from buyer to seller.* It's a complex syndrome: one part inertia, one part fear of the unknown, one part misplaced loyalty. Sometimes the leverage swing is triggered by forces outside the buyer's control. A third party—a government agency or an upstream customer in the supply chain—may certify only a few suppliers, or even just one. Or the vendor pool gets drained by marketplace attrition, leaving the last seller standing as a de facto sole source.

More typically, though, procurement professionals get squeezed into sole sourcing by internal factors:

- **Timing.** When a single bidder can meet the completion due date or start date, competition evaporates. The procurement team may lack adequate lead time to qualify other suppliers before their deadline.

- **Engineering.** Narrow specs—for raw material or finished products—may winnow out all but one approved vendor. In extreme cases, the buyer's engineers insert a lockout requirement that only their preferred supplier can meet. The sourcing manager is handcuffed. While the item may be one-of-a-kind, it's often a subjective or even inferior choice.

- **Fait accompli.** Certified legacy products are commonly designed-in. Starting from scratch with a different supplier may be seen as too costly or time-consuming. Such done deals are typical in the software market. Once an organization adopts a particular data format, a buyer will face stiff headwinds to get the company to switch.

- **Haste.** The sourcing department overcommits before gauging the supplier's performance and gets locked into an exclusive business cul-de-sac with no easy way out.

- **Inertia.** "We've always done it this way, so let's just keep things the same. It's easier on everyone."

- **Organizational preferences.** Internal business partners—engineering, marketing, senior management—tell you in so many words that seller A is the pick.

This last trap is especially pervasive. In a long-term buy-sell relationship, the vendor may feel like part of the furniture, if not part of the family. Over the years, it's natural for buy-side engineers or marketers to cozy up to their sole-source counterparts. The same goes for senior executives. They'll tend to balk at exploring other options, even after the supplier slides on performance or inflates their pricing. The procurement team may get blasted for suggesting a change. *How could we do that to Suzanne? Besides, just think of what might go wrong if we switch to somebody new!*

Larger organizations add another layer of complexity. Let's say Suzanne is hardworking and responsive, quick to find answers whenever the seller has an issue. Despite her best efforts, however, her company isn't performing up to snuff. Or maybe Suzanne is promoted and replaced by Steve, who's never around when you need him. The relationship slips and keeps on slipping, yet the buyer may shrink from voicing disappointment. Reliance on one supplier inhibits bargaining power. As points of contention are allowed to slide, both sides stop probing for ways to shave costs and add value.

Problems with a sole source rarely correct themselves. Left unconfronted, eroded performance standards and premium prices become the new normal. Unconditional cooperation obliterates competition. When buyers are reticent and sellers nonchalant, healthy business relationships go sideways. Deals get less productive. When creative conflict is jettisoned, both sides pay the price.

The Imperative of Vigilance

How can buyers get the upper hand—or at least rescue some equilibrium—in a sole-source negotiation? How can they know when a relationship should be renegotiated, reconsidered, or even ended? For starters, they need to do their homework—*before* it's time to reup a current deal. Did the supplier recently lose a big customer? Are they hawking an unproven version of their software in the marketplace? Do they have excess capacity after opening a new plant? Has a new competitor stepped on the scene?

The magic word is *vigilance*. When dealing with a sole source (or even a nonexclusive preferred source), a wise buyer stays alert for danger signs. Here are three red flags to monitor:

- **Stale products.** In competitive markets, you cannot compete without continuous changes, tweaks, and improvements. If a supplier delivers the identical product for eight or ten quarters running, especially in higher-tech, faster-moving fields, it's a sure sign of complacency.

- **Stale dynamics.** In new relationships, sole-source suppliers are founts of fresh ideas. They're generous with delight factors, and they find ways to make good things better. But once the honeymoon is in the rearview mirror, their ardor often cools. They stop trying so hard. When a buyer starts feeling taken for granted, they probably are.

- **Stale metrics.** In a thriving sole-source relationship, defect rates keep dropping. Cost reduction plans lower per-unit charges. Service response time and on-time completion rates continuously improve. When performance metrics are static, it's reason for concern.

When a sole source appears to be falling off, one useful tool is a "should cost" or clean-sheet analysis, which determines the true cost of any product or component. If a sole source is gouging, the clean sheet will tell the tale. Another reality check: market testing. Let's say you plan to stick with your sole source but want to keep them honest. You put your next contract out to bid to gauge the market and see what comes in. (A point of caution: If bidders know you're just fishing, they may aggressively underbid to embarrass the vendor of record or buy the business at a short-term loss.)

Finding Your Hidden Power

The hard fact is that *buyers have more power over sole sources than they believe.* As we've seen, human beings are painfully conscious of their own needs and vulnerabilities but less attuned to the stress points of others. When buyers feel anxious, they should ask themselves: What's going on with the supplier? How much of the account manager's quota depends on our business? Who might be pushing the salesperson from above?

Like anyone else, vendors are under fire to get deals done. Sole-source suppliers aren't so different from garden-variety sellers. They're at pains to protect existing business. They'll do whatever they can to preserve an established account.

To find their hidden leverage, buyers may need to resort to gamesmanship. At a seminar some years back, we met a purchasing manager named Alan from a Styrofoam cup manufacturer. After years in the business, they were down to one source for a specialty chemical. Alan told us how much he'd dreaded meeting with the chemical company's salesman. Each quarter came with a fresh price increase. As their bottom line took a beating, the buyer began tracking the supplier's raw costs. Here's what they found: When costs were flat, they got a price hike. When costs were *down,* they got a price hike. It was frustrating, but what could they do? Where else could they turn?

Then Alan had an idea, and his organization backed him. He gradually upped his orders of the chemical and stockpiled the surplus. Within a year, his company had amassed a three-month inventory. Alan was ready to make his move.

One fine day, the sales guy dropped by with his latest quote. Alan glared at it and said, "Another price increase! Well, you finally did it—you've priced yourself out of the market. You're way too high."

The salesman was stunned. "What do you mean?"

Alan said, "I can't give you the order."

"You've *got* to give me the order."

"No, I'm sorry, your price is just too high."

The next day the salesman came back, and for the first time in their long relationship, he cut his price. It wasn't a dramatic concession, just 2 percent off the prior day's number. But the conversation had a whole different tone. Alan sensed an advantage, and he stuck to his guns. "I'm sorry, but the price is still too high. I can't give you the order."

The salesman filed out in shock. The next day he slashed his price by 15 percent, with a shaky-voiced plea: "Am I competitive *now*?" Alan hadn't uttered a word about a rival source. But because he was sitting on a three-month stockpile, he could play a bluff—and it worked. The salesman was convinced that a new player must have broken into his marketplace. Phantom competition gave Alan as much leverage as the real thing.

Power is a matter of perception. It's subjective. If you believe you have leverage, and assert it with confidence, there's a fair chance the other side will fold—even when they're holding the stronger hand.

How to Get Your Mojo Back

Let's look at a few more strategies for buyers to get their mojo back. While none are guaranteed winners, all of them beat throwing up one's hands and saying, "What's the use? I'm just wasting my time trying to negotiate. I might as well close now at their asking price." In our experience, the facts on the ground rarely square with unconditional surrender. If a situation seems hopeless, it may be time to put on your game face and start thinking like a negotiator.

Even long-shot strategies have tactical value. Simply by planting the seed that there's another game in town, purchasers stand to gain leverage and push the seller onto their back foot. At the very least, the sole source will be reminded there are two sides to every deal.

Share the wealth. Is your sole source giving you a fair price, or are they taking advantage? You can't know for sure unless you test the waters. Before renewing a sole-source contract, buyers should review it stem to stern and identify what might be sourced elsewhere. With the advent of computer-aided design and manufacturing, barriers to entry are significantly lower than they used to be, even with highly specialized items. At minimum, your second source may be up to an ancillary role—for maintenance, say, or training or installation. When buyers float the possibility of going elsewhere, even for a small portion of the business, it may incentivize sellers to raise their game.

Before raising this at the table, it's recommended to run a cost-benefit analysis on alternative sources. If they're unable to meet the buyer's specs or have a poor reputation, the sole source could call your bluff. (And most likely they'll know—it's their turf, after all.) Here's a good general rule: Avoid making threats unless you're prepared to follow through.

Some companies hedge their bets by engaging a less proven supplier for a small percentage of the total contract, soup to nuts. Nothing keeps a preferred source on their toes more than an eager dual source. While smaller suppliers may be pricier, for lack of economies of scale, they may generate ideas for superior methods or technologies. A second line of communication is never a bad thing—it's like paying an insurance premium.

Meanwhile, the buyer will be helping to keep the dual vendor alive in the marketplace, just in case. As business trends toward greater dependence on fewer suppliers with less inventory, it's a C-suite priority to limit supply chain risk and potential revenue shortfalls. If the main source is struck by a force majeure (fire, hurricane, bankruptcy), the buyer can proceed to plan B. Even if the business you're giving the dual source doesn't amount to much, you're keeping their contact info handy.

Create an aura of competition. Say a prospective dual source isn't quite ready for primetime. There's no law against inviting them in for a friendly chat to see how their technology is progressing. Or from walking them out in full view of your long-term supplier's account manager, who just happened to be scheduled for the following meeting. It might get the sole source thinking: *Wait a minute, what are those guys doing here?*

Do it yourself. A variation on dual-source leverage, this strategy offers an added advantage. When a buyer floats a move to another vendor, the seller stands to have a good read on the competition and whether they're a real threat. But when it comes to a customer's internal capabilities, how can they know for sure? Even so, the same caveat applies: Don't threaten to go inside unless you're prepared to do just that. Empty threats will weaken your credibility in future negotiations.

Buy the sole-source company. The nuclear option. Though it may seem farfetched for smaller buyers, many companies grow through mergers and acquisitions. The most profitable targets are sole-source providers with competitive advantages and unique products or technologies.

Find a tech alternative. In an age of lightning-fast shifts in technology, it's always worth reviewing the state of play. Something new may be coming along that surpasses whatever the sole source is providing. Disruptive technologies, like 3D printing or rapid prototyping, can spill into any sector and transform it overnight. Consider the hotel industry (Airbnb), the taxi industry (Uber), the content distribution industry (Netflix), or the video conferencing business (Zoom). Even when a new technology is not quite appropriate to a customer's needs, or still in beta testing, the buyer can squeeze a sole source if plausible options may be coming onstream.

Test the second-hand market. The larger and more expensive a machine, the more vigorous the used market. (For software, the strategic equivalent would be to forgo an upgrade and stick with the older version instead.) Or the buyer might turn to a leasing company and rent the same machine. Either way, they'll gain leverage to negotiate a lower price on the new item.

Defer the deal. By postponing an agreement to the indefinite future, or simply dragging out the procurement process, buyers can often extract concessions. One of our clients was a big capital equipment provider. Boasting a 70 percent market share, they were the classic five-hundred-pound sole source gorilla. Given the astronomical cost of switching to a smaller supplier, customers were locked in tight. The provider seemed to hold all the cards. So why did they need a seminar on negotiating skills?

Here's why: those locked-in customers had figured something out. Four times a year, their sole source fell under enormous and predictable pressure. If the company blew its end-of-quarter numbers, its stock price would sag and salespeople would lose their bonuses. So the buyers did a dance. An excruciatingly slow dance. They'd be set to sign off on a large order, right up to the eleventh hour. Then they'd find some reason to cancel the meeting or phone call. Or they'd spot a snag in the fine print. Toward the end of March (or June, or September), the salespeople would panic and throw in all sorts of sweeteners to close their deals in time. The provider had no competition in the conventional sense, no secondary source stalking the sidelines. The salespeople were vulnerable to competitive stress and strain from *within* their organization. When the clock is ticking, sole sources get a lot more flexible.

Call the whole thing off. In today's belt-tightening environment, companies face unrelenting constraints to do more with less. There are countless potential projects but limited resources. Even multibillion-dollar corporations have budgetary constraints. We increasingly see companies shutting down product lines or abandoning whole business sectors.

As a result, a sole-source supplier—even one without credible competition—can find itself at risk. If the source is unreasonable, a buyer has the prerogative to walk away and seek a better return on investment elsewhere. The specter of cancellation is a potent motivator.

Divide and conquer. Most sales reps are careful to protect their reputations within their own firms. If a buyer gets stonewalled in a sole-source negotiation, they might break the ice by going over the rep's head—to the regional manager, the national account manager, even the VP of sales. In an extreme case, a buyer might ask for a new account manager. More often than not, these appeals will soften the most adamant supplier. Even when the buyer is a little fish, senior people may take a longer view of the relationship. If the buyer's business fails, after all, everybody loses.

Before going up the ladder, a buyer needs to ask: *Will the change be for the better? What are the chances they'll turn down our request? And what will our options be if they do?*

If and when a new account manager takes the reins, the buyer might offer some affordable concessions to get the new relationship off on the right foot. At the same time, they should return to the table with a wish list of items the previous manager rejected. The new person will be apt to be more pliable, since they'll be reluctant to jeopardize a preexisting relationship.

Pit the seller against themselves. When a product is truly one-of-a-kind, there may be little a buyer can do to get fairer prices or terms—in the short run. But over the longer haul, buyers have plenty of options, and the sole source needs to be made aware of them. Perhaps the item could be designed out in future models. Or the buyer could help establish a new startup or encourage a strategic partner to expand into the same arena. In a sense, you're pitting the seller's short-term profits against its long-term interests.

This strategy represents the best alternative to a negotiated agreement. Buyers going this route need to keep their end users in the loop and be willing to consider a plan B. They just might arrive at options they hadn't considered.

Carrots and Sticks

To this point, our sole-source strategies have invoked consequential leverage—the negative consequences for suppliers that refuse to make reasonable concessions. While fear is a powerful force, this approach has one big downside: It can damage or even wreck an important relationship.

When two parties share a high degree of trust, sole suppliers may be more effectively swayed through *positive* leverage. The simplest ways to sweeten a sole-source deal are to offer more business or a longer-term contract. A few other possible inducements from the buyer's side:

- A slot on the preferred suppliers list, giving the seller streamlined entrée to win new business. (The negative equivalent would be to move the seller to the "no new business" list.)

- A last look for new business, where the favored supplier is guaranteed the opportunity to beat the low bidder's price.

- The provision of good usage forecasts to enable the seller to make larger, more efficient production runs.

- A sharing of cost savings from joint value analysis or value engineering sessions.

- An introduction to other divisions in the buyer's firm as potential new customers. (Sweeter still is the prospect of entry to high-growth global markets.)

- Consideration of other items or new technologies in the seller's product line.

- Marketing support, including references, white papers, case studies, and demo sites.

In using positive leverage with a sole source, buyers aren't offering unconditional delight factors. In the spirit of creative dealmaking, they'll be seeking concessions in return. If a seller balks at a lower price or a volume discount, they might agree to a quid pro quo that costs them relatively little: additional consulting or free product samples, for example. The supplier might promise to get the buyer to market faster and generate revenue that much sooner, or to use vendor-managed inventory to reduce lead times and cut the buyer's inventory costs.

Which type of leverage is best? It's a case-by-case proposition. Some long-term relationships function so well that the carrot is all you need. In others, a two-pronged approach may work better. Say a buyer depends on a part from an erratic sole source. The buyer might say, "Look, we're considering giving you the order for a related part. But you're not going to get it until your quality control goes up and your pricing goes down." You're leveraging a potential status upgrade, contingent upon improvement.

The ideal ratio of carrots to sticks will hinge on your assessment of the other side. Some people genuinely believe that one good turn deserves another. That's the Brad and Rahman story. Others will take any overture as a sign of weakness and become even more inflexible. The market is probably your best gauge of the relationship. If the seller consistently delivers extra value over time, positive leverage makes sense. If they keep raising prices without adding value, it may be another story.

Either way, sole-source negotiations are not as hopeless as they may seem. Buyers need to remind themselves that they always have more cards to play. That mindset will help keep them on their front foot. In response, the sole source will be more inclined to stop, think, and negotiate in better faith.

Summary

- Sole sourcing can reduce transaction costs, strengthen accountability, and maximize creative tradeoffs.

- In a sole-source relationship, bargaining power naturally shifts from buyer to seller. If the seller's performance slips and the buyer is inhibited from confronting the problem, the benefits of the arrangement are lost.

- To restore equilibrium and keep sole sources on their toes, buyers can deploy a range of leveraging tools: should-cost analyses, market testing, sourcing parts of the contract elsewhere or in-house, going up the ladder to the sales rep's boss.

- Positive leverage will be more effective when it's tied to quid pro quo concessions from the other side.

12

Team Negotiations

Creative conflict is a team sport. It flowers in collaborative give and take, most obviously in internal negotiations. As deals swing from simple commodities to complex solutions, they contain more moving parts. It's one thing for a buyer to be handed a budget to upgrade the office's computer hardware. It's another to evaluate how a new system aligns with the company's legacy software, its value/price ratio, its networking needs, and its projected five-year growth. For organizational support, expertise, input, and feedback, stakeholder perspectives are invaluable. They lead negotiators to new options and help them target organization-wide priorities.

It's rare to find just one sourcing person at the bargaining table these days. Usually they're joined by at least two subject matter experts, plus a technical specialist from engineering or IT. Others have been consulted in the planning runup to the actual talks. Far from diluting the lead's power, cross-functional "tiger teams" can enhance a negotiator's authority and effectiveness.

Team negotiations straddle the internal and external. They tap into an organization's resources to strengthen its proposal to the other side. In any sphere involving complexity and uncertainty, according to James Surowiecki's *The Wisdom of Crowds*, groups are intrinsically smarter than the most brilliant individuals. From the futures market to the Super Bowl betting line, a high-functioning group makes better decisions than any isolated expert. The SARS virus, for example, was a collective discovery by eleven research labs in ten different countries. As Surowiecki says:

> That's why it's worthwhile to cast a wider net and why relying on a crowd of decision makers improves (though doesn't guarantee) your chances of reaching a good decision. . . .

> With most things, the average is mediocrity. With decision making, it's often excellence. . . . Under the right conditions, imperfect humans can produce near-perfect results.[1]

The same phenomenon can be observed in business negotiations. Setting a target price? Matching assets to needs? A cross-functional team can do it better than the most hyperskilled person on their own. There's a little more to it, however, than getting *x* people into a room together. Surowiecki acknowledges that not all crowds are wise. To perform reliably well, they must meet three criteria:

- **Diversity of opinion.** When groups are too homogeneous, they "find it harder to keep learning, because each member is bringing less and less to the table."[2] The ideal negotiating team ranges horizontally (across departments) and vertically (across hierarchies).

- **Independence from the influence of others.** Dissenting views add value. "You can be biased and irrational, but as long as you're independent, you won't make the group any dumber," Surowiecki says. "One key to successful group decisions is getting people to pay much less attention to what everyone else is saying."[3] To avoid groupthink, nurture a culture of autonomy.

- **Decentralization.** A decentralized team generates greater diversity of opinion. It also fosters specialization, which "tends to make people more productive and efficient," according to Surowiecki (and Adam Smith). "The closer a person is to a problem, the more likely he or she is to have a good solution to it."[4]

How do these ideas work in practice? In prenegotiation research on an RFP's low bidder, Joe from engineering talks informally to his counterpart on the vendor's side. Kate in marketing touches base with a competitor who hired the supplier last year. Elaine from legal combs court and business records to check for past litigation or other red flags. When they reconnoiter in the group, their assessments will be diverse, independent, and broadly decentralized—the three elements of smarter group decisions.

Team Principles

Cross-functional negotiating teams are customarily led by the organization's chief external negotiator, usually a sourcing or account manager. (In internal negotiations, a project manager may carry the ball.) While there are various styles for effective leadership, here are some all-weather guidelines:

- **Organize premeetings.** If a team meets for the first time at the negotiating table, you can't expect the members to know the plays. Someone might even score for the other side by mistake! An internal negotiation is an essential prelude to the external one.

- **Be inclusive, within reason.** The more constituencies represented on your team, the more credibility you'll gain across the organization. Surowiecki calls it "social proof," or "the tendency to assume that if lots of people are doing something or believe in something, there must be a good reason why."[5] Just as two heads are better than one, eight or ten heads can be better than three or four. The most effective team leaders recruit diverse skill sets, both creative types and more detail-oriented personalities—even though there may be friction between the two.

- **Take the mission in hand.** To gain internal acceptance, team leaders must project a clear vision for the deal's objectives. They might begin with a self-negotiation to determine what they want for their department and the company as a whole. Groups will be more cohesive when it's clear that their stated objectives can *only* be achieved collectively.

- **Persuade, don't dictate.** Skilled leaders stand up for their positions while staying open to new ideas. Don't monopolize the discussion, but freely speak your mind. As Surowiecki says, "If you talk a lot in a group people will tend to think of you as influential almost by default."[6] While not everyone is a natural master of persuasion, we can all deploy the following tactics, courtesy of Robert Cialdini:[7]

  - Establish your knowledge of the market before focusing on the deal.

  - Enlist peers to influence people horizontally, as opposed to top down. If veteran team members resist your direction, ask a respected old-timer for support.

  - Share exclusive information. You'll seize your stakeholders' attention when you say, "I just heard this today—it won't go public until next week."

- **Set your negotiation strategy in writing.** First, distinguish between the organization's "likes" and "musts"—between a perfect world and the bottom-line items you cannot live without. The two are often confused. A value mapping checklist will help address these questions:

  - What's our dream sheet, the solution that comes closest to meeting all of our needs? This sets the team's anchor and target positions.

  - What's the minimal solution we can accept? It's critical for team members to know the point where you'll walk away from the deal.

  - What's our BATNA?

  - Where does our side have leverage? Where are we vulnerable?

– What's our target deadline for closing the deal?

– What's our budget, and where is the money coming from? What departments can we draw on for cash, if needed?

- **Assign clear-cut roles.** Too many speakers can confuse or undercut your message. Who's going to kick off the external negotiation? Who will ask follow-ups after the other side presents? Who will observe but not talk at all? And before you get to the table: Who will dissect the deal's technical aspects? Who will look into the supplier's (or customer's) past history? Specific assignments make team members more invested and accountable.

- **Don't assume everyone gets it.** One of the best team leaders we know schedules a preplanning session weeks before the external negotiation. After distributing a detailed agenda, he lays out guidelines for when people should talk at the table, or not—and to watch for his signal to stop. (Should the other side propose a new wrinkle, they know better than to respond off the cuff.) Then he drills the group by asking individuals to describe the strategy. Once the external negotiation begins, he calls frequent caucuses to maintain a unified front. Nothing is left to chance.

- **Build a negotiating culture.** To reap benefits from the wisdom of crowds, tiger teams need real decision-making power. For the sake of creative conflict, the leader needs to prompt disagreement and encourage debate. Titles are checked at the door. As Adam Grant notes, "Dissenting opinions are useful *even when they're wrong.*"[8] By disrupting consensus, wrong ideas often lead to novel, superior solutions. And sometimes the wrong idea may turn out to be right, after all—but you'll never know unless the team gets to bat it around.

- **Overcome people's fear of ridicule.** Diverse viewpoints don't get heard when less assertive team members fear bucking the crowd. It's scary to be the lone naysayer. According to Heidi

Brooks of the Yale School of Management, effective team leaders "walk the talk."[9] They voice nonconforming ideas to encourage others to do the same. They prod people to throw spaghetti against the wall and see what sticks. Above all, they create a safe place for experimental thinking. They avoid dismissive judgments like: "That will never work." Instead, they might respond: "That's an interesting way of looking at it, and what if we tweaked it to do it this way?"

- **Be humble.** While arguing forcefully for their positions, team leaders must be willing to embrace a better idea, regardless of its source. A leader gains respect with three simple words: "I was wrong." Harry Truman said it best: "It is amazing what you can accomplish when you do not care who gets the credit."[10]

- **Don't rush to solutions.** Research shows that creative conflict is most valuable early on in a team's deliberations.[11] As Adam Grant points out, "When every member of a group has different information, inquiry needs to precede advocacy—which means you have to raise the problems before pursuing solutions."[12] At the outset of a premeeting, leaders need to elicit questions over answers, opinions before decisions.

The Benefits of Team Play

A more collective approach to business negotiations can pay substantial dividends. Consider the following advantages:

- **Broadened expertise.** Instead of one person deciding everything, teams tap into the wisdom of the group. They generate healthy challenges to the leader's choices: "Why did you pick that price? Why not a lower one?" Or: "That's a great narrative, but you never quantified our value."

Often the strongest experts come from within an organization. Others may be imported. Either way, they'll lend your claims more credibility. They'll also stiffen your spine when the other side bombards your position. A construction company might bring in a negotiating expert to sit in at the table and keep its team on the straight and narrow. Or they might invite an architect or a vendor with expertise on materials. The best hired guns meet Surowiecki's three criteria: diversity, independence, decentralization.

Don't overlook in-house senior management, who can bring a panoramic perspective. They'll know about the five other projects overlapping with yours and what that could mean for human resources and budgeting. But beware: the team will forfeit the wisdom of crowds if executives pull rank and inhibit disagreement.

- **Better planning.** Beyond adding resources, a team structure forces more concerted planning and discourages procrastination. People hold one another accountable. With expanded prep time and crowdsourced solutions, the lead negotiator can enlist various departments—accounting, engineering, research—to analyze the other side's needs and gauge their urgency to get the deal.

- **Firmer commitment.** Experiments show that we're more committed to targets set with others than ones established on our own. When braced by a collective, account managers are less likely to wobble and dip beneath an agreed-upon reserve price. If the other side throws a curveball, the lead negotiator can say, "Hold on, that sounds like it might be possible, but I'll need to caucus with my colleagues before giving you an answer." Teams are safety nets that catch you before you fall or correct you in real time: "Wait a second, Joe, we can't do that." Even when your teammates stay silent, their physical presence makes you less likely to fall prey to the emotions of the moment. (And if all else fails, somebody can kick you under the table.)

- **Relief.** There's nothing more exhausting than a marathon negotiating session, especially on deadline. When your energy flags, you'll be grateful for someone else to step in and carry the ball for a while.

- **Better listening.** When lead negotiators do all the talking, they can lose track of what they're saying or get distracted and miss an opening. Japanese business teams have a great fix: They appoint a designated listener and note-taker. In follow-up sessions, written notes will carry more weight than unsubstantiated recollections. (It's a good idea to take notes in your internal negotiations as well, to make sure that great ideas don't fall through the cracks.)

The Devil's Advocate

In the sixteenth century, the Vatican created a new job for one of their sharpest canon lawyers. It was the Renaissance version of opposition research. The appointee argued against prospects for sainthood by poking holes in reported miracles or slamming the candidate's character. Since this promoter of the faith faced off against advocatus Dei, God's advocate, he became known as *advocatus diabolic*—the devil's advocate.

Though we all know that every story has two sides, negotiators tend to get wedded to their positions. It's an automatic system problem. We fall in love with our own ideas and look for arguments that support them. We ignore holes in our logic and soldier on, blinders in place. Here's the rub: If we persist in seeing no evil, we leave ourselves more vulnerable to the other side's tactics.

Enter the modern-day devil's advocate, a team member who formulates conflict scenarios. McKinsey & Company has refined this into an art form. As their top negotiation expert told us, they "war game" for their clients. They listen to the company's procurement people and proceed to attack the stuffing out of them. Like a college debate or moot court, the exercise reveals weaknesses *before* the real negotiation, when the client still has time to shore them up.

Put another way, there's a big difference between *planning* (getting your facts and figures in a row) and *preparation* (knowing what to do when the other side shoots holes in your carefully planned presentation). Preparation is the best antidote to complacency. It forces team members to cull out soft spots in the leader's approach. In *Thinking, Fast and Slow*, Daniel Kahneman touts the "premortem" used by psychologist Gary Klein, Kahneman's "adversarial collaborator":

> The procedure is simple: when the organization has almost come to an important decision but has not formally committed itself, Klein proposes gathering for a brief session a group of individuals who are knowledgeable about the decision. The premise of the session is a short speech: "Imagine that we are a year into the future. We implemented the plan as it now exists. The outcome was a disaster. Please take 5 to 10 minutes to write a brief history of that disaster."[13]

Effective devil's advocates need to think like negotiators. They must anticipate the trash the other party will throw on your lawn. In the best case, they'll open the negotiation to a broader exchange of ideas, to fresh ways of looking at the deal and a more creative, better-for-both outcome.

Team Negotiation Pitfalls

While the rewards far outweigh the risks, negotiating as part of a group is not without pitfalls. Consider:

- **Lowest common denominator.** A meritocracy is not a democracy. You're striving for a no-holds-barred search for the best idea, not a bland consensus. If team leaders downplay disagreement, creative friction will be muffled. If they strain to keep everybody happy, the team can't innovate or add value. As Surowiecki notes, "The search for consensus encourages tepid lowest-common-denominator solutions which offend no one rather than exciting everyone."[14]

- **The all-knowing leader.** When the team leader is imperious, thin-skinned, vindictive, or simply in too big a hurry, others will be reluctant to question the leader's position. In accordance with social norms, they'll submerge valid differences so as to get along. Hierarchy erodes the wisdom of the crowd.

- **Disunity at the table.** In every team negotiation, there comes a point where the divergent thinking of creative conflict must yield to *convergent* behavior, a united front. If your teammates veer off in three directions while you're going hammer and tong with the other side, you've got a problem. Rogue dissenters are especially bad news. They'll raise the other party's expectations and encourage them to dig in.

Say you're leading the selling side and the buyer asks, "So how long will it take to do this change, and how much will it cost?" Before you can get a recess to caucus, your team's tech expert blurts out, "About three weeks and $100,000." Or maybe he volunteers, "Oh, that takes no effort at all, we'll just throw it in and have it done by Monday." While he may have no special knowledge of pricing or scheduling, his estimate will be hard to walk back.

An ill-disciplined team is where leverage goes to die.

- **A soft devil's advocate.** In the 1991 comedy film, *Defending Your Life*, Albert Brooks plays an advertising executive named Daniel Miller who's about to negotiate his salary at his new firm. The night before, he asks his wife to help him prepare.

    Wife: What do you want me to do?

    Daniel: Be him.

    Wife: This is silly.

    Daniel: It's not silly, it helps me. Offer me $55,000, no more.

    Wife: How much do you want?

    Daniel: How much are you offering me?

    Wife: $55,000.

    Daniel: I can't work here for a penny under sixty-five, I'm sorry.

    Wife: Well, I can't pay you sixty-five.

    Daniel: Then I can't work here.

Wife: $58,000.

Daniel: Sixty-five.

Wife: Fifty-nine?

Daniel: Sixty-five.

Wife: Sixty?

Daniel: (Emphatically.) Sixty-*five*.

Wife: Sixty-one.

Daniel: Let me make it plain. I cannot take the job for under sixty-five, under no conditions.

(*The following afternoon, Daniel goes in to see his prospective boss.*)

Boss: Daniel, I'm prepared to offer you $49,000.

Daniel: (*Extending his hand to shake.*) I'll take it!

Boss: (*Happily surprised.*) I'm going to get you a parking place.

Daniel: (Dejected, knowing he's blown it.) Okay.

- **Daniel had no problems holding firm with his wife.** But when push came to shove, he couldn't defend his position. Adam Grant would tell you he lost the game at his practice session: "For devil's advocates to be maximally effective, they need to really believe in the position they're representing—and the group needs to believe that they believe it, too."[15] Daniel's wife played her role without conviction. As a result, Daniel came into the real talks with false confidence. That's a deadly handicap at the table.

- **Groupthink.** Confirmation bias, the unconscious tendency to seek out information that supports our existing beliefs, obliterates the wisdom of crowds. A tragic case in point is the 2003 space shuttle *Columbia* disaster. Not long after blastoff, a piece of foam broke off the fuel tank and clipped the orbiter's wing. In lock-step with its leader, NASA's

Mission Management Team (MMT) dismissed the notion that the foam strike could be fatal. As a result, some high-risk but plausible options—a potential rescue mission or an in-orbit repair—weren't even considered. The *Columbia* disintegrated upon reentry, killing all seven crew members. The MMT's performance, Surowiecki says, sadly illustrated how small groups can make bad decisions:

> Rather than begin with the evidence and work toward a conclusion, the team members worked in the opposite direction. . . . Even when MMT members dealt with the possibility that there might be a real problem with *Columbia*, their conviction that nothing was wrong limited discussion and made them discount evidence to the contrary.[16]

- **When people fall back on common assumptions or defer to rigid systems, fresh ideas are stunted.** Negotiating teams are no panacea. Research shows that a "tendency to remain silent rather than express a difference exists both in individual relationships and in groups, where we fear a loss of status or even expulsion if we differ from the rest. . . . We do what we believe other group members want us to do. We say what we think other people want us to say."[17]

- **Loose lips.** The tactical imperative for discretion takes on added urgency in a team context, where there are more potential leaks in the run-up to the talks. The guilty parties tend to be smart, competent, and loyal—and unschooled in the art of negotiating. Engineers are among the most notorious offenders. If they like the supplier's tech person, they may inadvertently let slip something like, "Your competitor's product didn't work worth a damn." Or: "Congratulations, you guys are the only ones who passed the acceptance test!" Or: "Thank God you'll be working with us, you're the only ones who can meet our deadline." These people are just trying to be helpful. It never crosses their mind that they've shredded your leverage.

To plug leaks before they start, leaders can stress the need for discretion and ask their teammates to spread the word to their departments: "The less the other side knows about our company's business, the better off we are." This doesn't mean people can't talk to their counterparts. It does mean that they need to think strategically and *choose* what they divulge.

Conversely, team leaders might ask their people to pump the other side for information. Reconnaissance can be gathered by just about anyone, even executive assistants. This tactic is more effective well in advance of the negotiation, perhaps over a friendly lunch, before the other party's antennae are up. *How does your company do sales forecasting? How long have you been working for the same boss? How's business going for you right now?* These seemingly innocent questions can deliver a handsome payoff down the road. Handled with care, discovery can be a team sport, too.

Summary

- Winning negotiating teams share three characteristics: diversity of opinion, decentralization, and a culture of autonomy and free dissent.

- Before engaging the other side, internal negotiations are a must for clarifying roles and laying out the team strategy.

- Effective team leaders assert their own positions while creating a safe space for contrary views. When a better idea emerges, they don't hesitate to change course.

- To prepare for the other side's attacks, appoint a devil's advocate to poke holes in the team's approach.

- As the team moves from planning to the actual negotiation, make sure that everyone is on the same page. If your team seems divided at the table, the other side will conquer.

13

Internal Negotiations

In most organizations, the lion's share of negotiating—as much as 70 percent, according to our clients—is internal. Whenever you meet with your boss, you're entering an undeclared negotiation. Ditto for seemingly innocent conversations with your direct reports or other business units. In unstructured settings, it can be hard to discern exactly where you are on the continuum. You might be haggling to put out a fire and at the same time seeking a better long-term arrangement for both parties.

With all of its moving parts and ambiguity, the internal sphere has one constant: *Relationships are primary.* The people you're dealing with this week are likely to be there next month and next year. It's rarely in your interest to make internal enemies. Any short-lived rewards won't be worth the risk.

In the modern workplace, top-down hierarchies have given way to horizontal or diagonal dotted-line networks. Dictates have yielded to agreements, and agreements must always be negotiated. *How can we work things out to our mutual advantage, and to the benefit of the organization as a whole? How do we make a deal that's better for both and even optimal for all?* Creative conflict lies at the beating heart of this change.

It might seem reasonable to assume that internal negotiations are less stressful than external ones. For one thing, you're likely to know your counterparty going in. You might consider them friends. After all, you're on the same team, pulling on the same oar, pointed in the same direction—aren't you? It should be a snap to get on the same page—right?

In reality, internal negotiations can be the most difficult of all. Whether you're a buyer or seller, you'll be obliged to sell your strategies to cross-functional team members and a gauntlet of other business units, not least of all the C-suite. For sourcing and account managers alike, internal buy-in is an unwritten job requirement. Consider all the people that may need to be brought on board:

- **Engineering/technical.** These spec-driven professionals will set their sights on their gold standard—the tech with all the bells and whistles. Then they'll tell you, "We picked who we want, just go and ink the deal."

- **Finance.** As budgetary gatekeepers, they'll urge you to watch your spend. You'll spend weeks to locate the perfect vendor, only to hear, "The financial impact is too great, find another source."

- **Legal.** Also known as the sales prevention team, they're perfectly capable of stalling a contract indefinitely to pressure the customer into more favorable terms and conditions . . . or to eliminate the smallest theoretical shred of liability.

- **Marketing.** "Since we're the ones who have to sell this stuff, you've got to give us what we need."

- **Senior management.** "My friend at ABC Inc. just called with a complaint. He said they weren't treated fairly in the bidding process—and that we're making a big mistake by going with XYZ."

Closer Is Harder

The closer the two parties, the tougher the negotiation—especially when they have a checkered history. The past distorts the present and shadows the future. A single negative experience—no matter how ancient—can incline an internal partner to derail you the next time around. Dysfunctional relationships play out according to script—if it was written by Edward Albee.

You're always making decisions without me.

And you're the one always holding up the show.

Why do you always harp on that?

Every organization has its outsiders, to paraphrase David Brooks, otherwise known as knee-jerk curmudgeons. But while open antagonism is a destructive force, most internal negotiators—like negotiators in general—err on the side of acceptance or avoidance. They give in or give up. Say you and your colleague enjoy having lunch together, or maybe you play on the company softball team. Who wants to fight within the family? Our social norms lead us to swallow our differences, especially with people we know to be sensitive or short-tempered. To avoid bruising someone's ego, we shut off debate before it can lead to something fruitful. We get stuck in tacit stalemates. Each party perceives the other as the obstacle. What's worse, neither is willing to say so openly.

As one sourcing professional acknowledged, "I'd much rather deal with a vendor than with my internal end user. If a vendor gets upset with me, it's no big deal—that's part of my job. But if my internal client gets upset, they'll find a way to get back at me." To avoid giving offense, people sidestep sticky issues like enforcement or postdeal accountability. They become magical thinkers, hoping for the best.

We've seen how conflict avoidance squelches value-adding solutions. Internally, it also does a number on an organization's integrity. At the height of the dot-com bubble, corporations beset by scandal—Tyco, Enron, WorldCom, Arthur Andersen—were infamous for their hypercompliant boards. *Harvard Business Review* met the moment with a celebrated article that decried our reticence culture: "Is Silence Killing Your Company?"[1]

> The social virtues of silence are reinforced by our survival instincts. Many organizations send the message—verbally or nonverbally—that falling into line is the safest way to hold on to our jobs and further our careers. . . .

But it is time to take the gilt off silence. Our research shows that silence is not only ubiquitous and expected in organizations but extremely costly to both the firm and the individual. Our interviews with senior executives and employees in organizations ranging from small businesses to *Fortune* 500 corporations to government bureaucracies reveal that silence can exact a high psychological price on individuals, generating feelings of humiliation, pernicious anger, resentment, and the like that, if unexpressed, contaminate every interaction, shut down creativity, and undermine productivity. . . .

Silence does not have to be about fraud and malfeasance to do grave damage to a company. All too often, behind failed products, broken processes, and mistaken decisions are people who chose to hold their tongues rather than to speak up. Breaking the silence can bring an outpouring of fresh ideas from all levels of an organization—ideas that might just raise the organization's performance to a whole new level.

Our aim of this chapter is to help you turn internal roadblocks into opportunities. To begin with, you'll need a new orientation. Where external negotiators are wise to begin at the left pole of the continuum, as bargainers, and then move to the right as warranted, internal negotiators should aim for the right end from the start. The priority is to build a bond that can grow into a long-term strategic alliance. If the other person proves unreliable or unready, you can usually pull back to a less trusting mode without much harm done.

As we've noted, competition remains alive and well in relationship-building. But competition doesn't have to equate to combat. On the give-and-take spectrum, internal negotiators are characteristically matchers. It's reasonable to keep score, within reason, and to expect reciprocation. As in all relationships, internal negotiators must stay vigilant to follow up, enforce, and monitor the agreement—to keep the other side honest.

Strong internal relationships don't happen spontaneously. They must be built. When steps are skipped, people pay a high price. After one seminar, a Microsoft engineer approached us and confided, "You know, I work fast and efficiently. If others come to me for answers, I help them. I've been the top performer in my department for years, but less experienced people keep getting promoted ahead of me. And now I realize it's because I never put in an effort to develop relationships with my colleagues. I thought it was enough to do my job well. I never tried to understand what *they* were doing and how we fit together."

Watch Your Step

Landmines are legion in internal negotiations, on both the sales and sourcing sides.

Drifting into Trouble

In external negotiations, it's obvious when you're bargaining over a price or hammering out terms and conditions. But what about these situations?

- *I checked in with operations, and they say that minor change my customer wants is impossible.*

- *I ran into Joan from legal in the corridor and told her we need more flexibility with our T's & C's or we'll never get this contract signed.*

- *Just got an email from marketing. They want to push up the delivery date to launch their new campaign a month early.*

We tend to pass off these encounters as everyday office interactions. In fact, each of them is a negotiation—loosely structured, on the fly, but a negotiation nonetheless. If you fail to recognize that fact, you'll lose an opportunity to advance your interests. You'll be on your back foot without even knowing it.

Priorities and Constraints

Even when all hands are aligned with the organization's mission, people will differ over how best to make it happen and what matters most. It's hard enough to flush out their technical requirements to understand what they need from the deal. It's tougher still to meet their subjective needs and move them from frustration to satisfaction.

The daylight between external negotiators and their internal stakeholders is rooted in the divergent ways they are measured. It's essentially a silo problem. For sourcing managers, the key performance indicator is usually price-based cost savings. But a great price won't help an operations manager who gets rated by output or runtime. How do we bring these metrics into sync? Senior management can help by shifting to weighted measurements. Beyond pricing, buyers should consider on-time delivery, support, defect rate, extended payment terms, and all the various elements that figure into total cost of ownership. In the real world, however, costs and benefits are never shared equally in any one transaction. Some stakeholders may need to make extra concessions while trusting they'll get added consideration the next time around. That's where a healthy relationship will make all the difference.

When faced with sharp differences, stakeholders may be tempted to soft-soap the conflict, rubber-stamp a marginally acceptable agreement, and hope to fix it down the road: "Okay, I'll live with anything you give me, just get me out of this mess." Or they may jump into antagonistic conflict: "Either you give me what I want or I'll go over your head." Either way, an opportunity for creative conflict has been lost.

Unintended Consequences

Whenever an external negotiation moves beyond simple tradeoffs and into more advanced creative dealmaking, there's apt to be internal blowback—on both sides. What seemed like a no-brainer for the executive team may raise utter havoc a few layers down, among those most directly affected. If they had no input into the deal, the fallout can be radioactive.

For instance, your vendor agrees to accept progress payments fifteen days after the start of each phase of the project. And your accounts payable manager says: "Are you kidding me? We have an automated payment system. Now I'll have to assign someone to monitor this vendor's activity and create a special manual system just for them. That makes no sense."

Or say you've saved some money and have done the vendor a favor by assenting to a new packaging and distribution format. But no one's consulted the retail store managers, and one of them shoots back an angry email: "It may not have occurred to you, but now we'll have to juggle every single shift schedule. And where's the extra support we'll need to retrain our people? Did anyone think of that?"

Sourcing groups may orchestrate a handful of big deals per year. Their next raise or promotion may ride on a single outcome. But once a contract is signed, they move on. It's a different story for their stakeholders, who must live with the results and, what's more, be measured by them. If sourcing made a bad choice, their department could be compromised. The dynamic is inherently conflicting.

The Fait Accompli

In deals involving repeat business, the buyer's end users will build close relationships with their counterparts on the vendor's side— sometimes too close. It's not uncommon for buyers to be blind-sided by a de facto agreement and forced at gunpoint to sign it. Often these deals will lack synergies and fall short of comprehensive solutions. Tight deadlines tend to leave little or no room for revision or flexibility. Hence the buyer's age-old complaint: "They don't tell me until I hear they need it yesterday."

"You Don't Need to Know"

Old-school end users view purchasing through a twentieth-century lens—as a nuts-and-bolts procurement process where the buyer simply inks the contract after the end users craft the deal. They may hoard information as a power move, or to enable them to step in and save the day after the buyer screws up. "We've always done it like this," they'll lecture the purchasing professional. "There's no other way—you just don't understand." When a fait accompli is dressed up as a modus operandi, the damage can be lasting. While turf warriors eventually beat themselves, they can take the buyer—and the company—down with them.

Internal Warfare

Let's flash back to our thin client server negotiation in chapter 7. It's two days before Jackson, the sourcing specialist for International Distributors, has his sit-down with Lesley from High Performance Systems. He's already decided that he wants to go with her. But first he dutifully meets with Rose, his freshly promoted network manager. He soon discovers that his internal client has a very different view of the deal.

> Jackson: Rose, we've given a long look at all five companies that responded to our RFP. Based on our analysis, we think High Performance Systems is by far the best choice. They've got a ten-year track record for quality work and on-time delivery. Their service is topnotch. If we accept their bid, we'll all be able to sleep at night.
>
> Rose: Good lord, are you kidding me? Did you see their price tag? Look, I happen to know a little something about local area networks. Good Enuf is more than good enough. They'll give us a perfectly satisfactory product at a far better price.
>
> Jackson: Wow, I'm surprised to hear you say that. With due respect, I'm afraid I have to disagree. This is a big job—too big for a young company like Good Enuf. And Joan in operations really wants that High Performance dashboard feature. She says it'll make her job a lot easier.

Rose: I like Joan, but it's not her call. We don't need all the bells and whistles, and quite frankly we can't afford them. Our absolute top should be $300,000.

Jackson: I'm not sure that price can get us a reliable vendor—and isn't that what counts most for your engineers?

Rose: Look, I'm the customer here. I appreciate your input, but we both know you've had your issues in the tech area in the past, right? My mind is made up on this one, and I'm pretty certain the VP of operations agrees with me. I need you to sign with Good Enuf and get their system up and running ASAP. We're going live in four weeks. So . . . (*Weighty pause.*) Are we good?

Poor Jackson! He's just demonstrated how *not* to handle an internal negotiation. Rose came armed with zero-sum bargaining tactics: flinching, trash talking, a tactical deadline. To top it off, she flaunted her superior expertise and invoked a higher power. Jackson drifted into the process with next to no planning or data. When Rose torpedoed his plan, he was caught flat-footed. He had no idea why Rose felt so strongly about Good Enuf. He was taken aback by her skepticism about High Performance—and her dismissiveness toward Jackson's judgment. Was it something he said? Or was Rose just a professional pain in the neck?

As we can see, internal negotiations carry huge ramifications for buyers, their stakeholders, and their organizations. The same holds true for account managers and salespeople. A failure to coordinate sales strategy can lead to unplanned concessions—like expedited delivery or accelerated software updates—and a bitter dispute with their manufacturing or tech people. Many a promising career has crashed and burned after a wrongfooted negotiation on a critical account.

Now that we've laid out the challenges and pitfalls in this arena, let's consider a five-point program to reach agreements that are optimal for all.

1. Build Rapport

In business as in life, dealings go more smoothly when we have a strong relationship going in. In building rapport with an internal coworker, you're preparing for *tomorrow's* negotiation, for problems not yet on the horizon. You're hoping to bank some goodwill. Later on, when *you* need cooperation, the other side will be more likely to reciprocate.

If you have a poor relationship or none at all going in, you'll need to spend time to fix or build it. Ideally, you'll get to know your internal colleague *before* the two of you are faced with a tough decision or pressing deadline. In choosing the right time and place to talk, neutral territory is best. Sharing coffee and donuts in a conference room might do in a pinch, but people will be more relaxed at lunch or while grabbing a drink after work. When lining up an especially important ally, consider taking them to dinner.

At the outset, it's usually better to defer shop talk and open with small talk, or nontask talk. There's gold to be mined in topics like family, hobbies, favorite TV shows, or sports teams. (Politics can be trickier, unless you know going in that the two of you broadly agree.) The goal is to come to see each other not as inputs and outputs in a work process but as people with similar interests or values. A bit of mutual admiration goes a long way, as Robert Cialdini points out:

> Managers can use similarities to create bonds with a recent hire, the head of another department, or even a new boss. . . . The important thing is to establish the bond early because it creates a presumption of goodwill and trustworthiness in every subsequent encounter. It's much easier to build support for a new project when the people you're trying to persuade are already inclined in your favor.
>
> Praise, the other reliable generator of affection, both charms and disarms. Sometimes the praise doesn't even have to be merited. . . . Experimental data show[s] that positive remarks about another person's traits, attitude, or performance reliably generates liking in return, as well as

willing compliance with the wishes of the person offering the praise.[2]

Once a social foundation is established, it's time to learn about the other person's work style. Do they prefer one-page summaries, or do they like to be involved every step of the way? Beyond the scope of the next deal, what problems are they facing at work? You can also take the opportunity to explain the subtleties of your role. You might clarify the department's goals or how your performance is measured. This will enable a coworker to appreciate the basis of your concerns or your reluctance to just "go along."

At some point, differences will surely surface between you and your new best friend. But a strong rapport will make them more easily reconciled, whether by finding a ZOPA or shifting into creative dealmaking. Once a real relationship is established, and you're comparing notes on your favorite series on Netflix, you'll be on the road to a resilient business partnership.

2. Early Involvement

Heading into an external negotiation, it's vital to engage any and all internal stakeholders. When people feel they were sold down the river with no input, they may undermine the deal. If problems crop up later on, they'll have little incentive to go the extra mile to make the agreement work: "You didn't talk to me then, but you're coming to me now?"

To avoid internal tension, sound the stakeholder out: *How would this contract affect you and your team?* Since you'll know more about the overall deal, be patient in laying out the facts. At the same time, you should also be prepared for the other person to see those facts in a different light.

Timing is everything in internal negotiations. The process must begin long before the external deal is done. If you wait until after you've narrowed the field to A or B, it may be too late to ask, "Which do you prefer?" Many end users will want you to walk back the process two or three steps. And some will say, "But what about C?"

Consulting with stakeholders is more than a pro forma exercise. Often they'll add value by catching something you overlooked. Say your company is upgrading its routers and you think you've found the best possible company with the lowest price. Your tech person scans a contract draft and asks, "Who's going to support the legacy technology?" In moments like these, a collaborative process can save a sourcing manager's skin.

It's impossible to please everybody. But when you bring people into a negotiation upfront, rather than treating them as afterthoughts, it makes a big difference. It's one thing to tell someone, "Okay, I know you like option A over option B, but it just makes too much sense to go with B. You'll have to live with it." You'll send a very different message by saying, "Look, we know you like A, but it makes so much sense to go with B. What else can we do in this deal to help you live with B?" In the spirit of creative conflict, you're acknowledging your differences to find a better outcome. Treated with respect, the end user will be more inclined to help make the deal work—and to keep sharing their candid opinions the next time around.

One more thing: it helps to deliver a disappointing verdict by phone, if not face-to-face. Brusque emails have poisoned many a relationship.

Early involvement cuts both ways, of course. When approached for a last-second sign-off, your first order of business is to review the process and investigate why you weren't brought into the loop earlier on. Do some nonjudgmental fact-finding: *Tell me how you arrived here. Did you consider any other options? What made this one stand out?* If colleagues balk at revisiting these issues, remind them that it's your responsibility to understand the agreement before you can put your name to it.

Before signing off, try to inject some eleventh-hour value and salvage a better outcome. It won't be easy. With a done-deal agreement, the other side will dig in and stand their ground. They'll resist further concessions—especially on price, where any proposed change may come off as an unsavory nibble, if not an out-and-out escalation.

Still, there may be room to maneuver. You can still ask: *What else can we look at? What creative opportunities haven't been considered? Are there broader possibilities in this deal?* Late in the game, your leverage may be limited, but it's still greater than zero. The deal won't go through until you say yes.

As you attempt to forge last-minute improvements, you may strike out. Nonetheless, it's worth trying. By reminding your colleagues of the value that you and your department bring to the process, you're setting the stage for the next negotiation. Over time, coworkers will come to see you as an asset rather than a barrier. They'll start thinking: *Maybe I should have brought this person in a little sooner.*

3. Discovery

The 90-10 rule applies here in spades. The most pervasive mistake in internal negotiations is the failure to get enough information beforehand. When we commit 90 percent of our time to investigating our stakeholders' needs (as opposed to their *wants*), the investment saves untold hours and headaches down the road. It also helps us reality-check inflated expectations—our own, included. Along the way, we build credibility by keeping an eye out for bigger-picture opportunities for a broader deal.

The fundamental tools of discovery are questions, including the so-called dumb ones. Beyond clarifying technical information, savvy internal negotiators are thirsty for insights into the stakeholder's thought process. When an engineer declares that you need to buy *this* brand of gadget and no other, or "we have to do it *that* way," you can't just take their word for it. And so you ask:

- Walk me through this. Can you help me understand what's special about your preference?

- What are the other top options? Why aren't they as good?

- If you have a problem after the deal is signed, how will this vendor support you? What are the consequences if they fail to meet the agreed-upon service level?

- Is there anything else the vendor might be able to do for us that we haven't asked for yet?

- If we do it this way instead, what can go wrong?

Lawyers are notorious for their intimidating jargon and hard-bargaining tactics—it's what they do for a living. You should expect them to be no less aggressive when negotiating internally. They'll refuse to make first concessions and resort freely to TIOLIs. Even when they have wiggle room to spare, they'll reflexively start at *no*.

In response, a buyer or salesperson should be respectful but persistent and rigorously well-prepared. To enlist support from legal, it helps to defer to their expertise and their obligation to protect the company's interests. At the same time, you'll be subtly reminding them that *you* are the business expert. And business matters, even for lawyers. It keeps their lights on.

Emotion will get you nowhere with attorneys. Only logic can carry the day. Say a proposed contract comes back heavily red-lined. To uncover a veiled agenda or challenge a dubious rule, you might prepare a line of questions:

- Why are people objecting to this clause? Is it a language problem or a content problem?

- Help me understand something: What's the purpose of indemnification in this context?

- What does "unlimited liability" mean? Why do we feel so strongly about it? Have things ever gone wrong in this area? Is it possible we're overprotecting ourselves?

If legal stays stuck in *no* mode, don't assume you're at an impasse. Say the sticking point is over lending the company's good name to a joint marketing effort. "We simply never do that," the lawyer says. But you keep probing:

- Have we ever made an exception? What were the circumstances?

- Given our company's needs in the marketplace, how could we approach this one differently?

- Do we have any flexibility? Where do you think there might be room for compromise?

- And again: Is there a different way to approach this?

For more traction, it can be helpful to float a possible fix: *What if we did it this way?* Even if your solution fails to pass muster, it might provoke some useful brainstorming. Here's a real-world case: A stakeholder from finance was pressing a sourcing leader named Raquel to consolidate suppliers through an RFP and toss out those who came in high. It seemed entirely logical, save for one thing. No one had anticipated the possibility that *all* of the favored suppliers would miss the cut. Raquel embarked on a pointed voyage of discovery: *Do we have a ramp-down plan? Do we have a BATNA? In the worst case, what are our options?* By revealing the hidden costs that lurk in any strategic sourcing initiative, Raquel led her company to devise a modified strategy with downside protection.

In-depth discovery soaks up time, a scarce resource. But once you make it a habit, the benefits will be profound—if not for the current deal, for the next one.

Three final points on discovery:

- To get your stakeholders thinking more creatively, try asking: *If you could start this process/project from scratch, how would you do it?*

- If you encounter internal resistance, consider enlisting a devil's advocate.

- To avoid future misunderstandings, keep a contemporaneous record of all communications. That thirty-second phone call or passing hallway exchange can come back to bite you if the two parties remember it differently. Written notes can be lifesavers, particularly if your end user leaves the company or shifts to a different job.

4. Forewarning

In internal negotiations, forewarning takes one of two forms. The first is to let your stakeholders know early on what may be coming in the external talks. It's a natural part of the discovery process: *Here's what we're thinking of doing, tell me how that would affect you. Do you have other ideas we might try?*

Keeping people in the loop is your best defense against unintended consequences and ruptured trust. It can also help prevent costly mistakes. Say you scored a 20 percent discount on a work station order simply by agreeing to change the color of the desk from cobalt blue to lime green. When you belatedly get around to notifying the vice president of marketing, he tells you, "We tried that color before and it just sat on the shelf—it's a loser." Oops!

The thinner your track record with the stakeholder, the more deliberate these heads-ups need to be. As you build a stronger working relationship, your business partners will naturally give you more rein.

A second type of forewarning is a framework for flagging post-contractual problems. Sourcing managers make commitments to their internal clients based on commitments from suppliers. If the supplier later nibbles on the agreement, the sourcing manager has effectively let down the end user. Likewise, the supplier's account manager has been disappointed by their operational team's poor performance. Worst of all, both sides may be unaware of any problems on the ground until they've mushroomed into a full-blown crisis.

Say you've signed a software deal. A year later, your engineers are insisting that the agreed-upon spec is outmoded. Meanwhile, the vendor was unable to get the promised 24/7 access to the buyer's system. Now their ops people are screaming at the account manager: "We've given away too much work, we've got to start charging more for it!" When a vendor holds most of the leverage and is willing to resort to brinksmanship, your options are limited. All you may be able to do is to negotiate slightly better terms for the change.

To head these disasters off at the pass, tell your internal client up front, "Look, we've made a great deal, but some things probably won't go the way they're mapped out. If you see anything going south, I want you to bring it to my attention right away. And I'll do the same for you."

5. Negotiate!

Looked at objectively, internal negotiations should offer less risk and more reward than the external variety. Subjectively, they can be capsized by all-or-nothing power struggles: Either we win the internal stakeholder around to our position or the other party beats us. But if we're thinking like negotiators, our differences can point us toward more creative solutions. We can hunt together for an agreement that adds value for all.

As their organization's negotiation experts, sourcing specialists and account managers need to take the lead in surfacing disagreements. Internal transactions require the same level of planning and preparation as external deals. Before sitting down with your stakeholders, ask yourself: *Where do I have leverage? What's my starting anchor? My fallback position? The minimum I'll accept? And what can I ask for in return?*

Since they're starting on the far right of the continuum, in relationship-building mode, internal negotiators might offer to split the difference—or even make the first concession—to get the ball rolling and set a reciprocal tone. A harmonious relationship will more than compensate for what you've conceded.

That doesn't mean seeking agreement at any price, however. When your colleague repeatedly ignores a deadline, you may turn to consequential leverage and say, "If you don't get me those specs by the end of the week, I'll need to go to your boss." But that's a last resort, and it can easily backfire. Positive leverage is the internal tool of choice.

Despite your best efforts, some colleagues may fail to see the value of internal negotiation. Others may see no point in talking to you at all. Nonetheless, your mission is to persevere and keep prodding your coworkers for information and feedback. The alternative—giving in to frustration and flying solo—is a recipe for resentment. The best negotiators sustain a long-term, wide-angle outlook. The good of the organization comes first and last.

Creative conflict is not the easy road. It's simpler to wrangle over price than to try to broaden a complex transaction. Senior management may gently prod a sourcing specialist to the left on the continuum: "You don't have to hit a home run. If you can do slightly better on the price, that's good enough." The same message can be conveyed on the seller's side: "Nudge the price up just a little bit, and you're done." Squeezed by deadlines, negotiators may hold back from broaching broader solutions. Why make things more intricate when everybody just wants you to close? But as Perlow and Williams note, "When we perpetually silence ourselves in the short-sighted belief that we are getting our tasks done as expeditiously as possible, we may interfere with creativity, learning, and decision making."[3] Unchecked consensus is an organizational deathtrap.

Internal and external negotiations are intertwined. When negotiators dive into creative conflict with their stakeholders, they gain more room to maneuver with the outside party as well. When you're confident that you'll get a fair hearing from your colleagues, you feel more freedom to probe for a better, broader deal. But before engaging the external party, you need to enlist *your* side first.

Now let's return to Jackson's negotiation with Rose, his new network manager—but this time in a happier parallel universe. Long before the two meet, Jackson takes the trouble to call a friend who worked with Rose at her last job. He learns that she was sabotaged by a buyer who'd steered a contract to his old college roommate. Rose's company wound up paying a premium for shoddy performance. "It probably cost her a promotion," Jackson's friend tells him. "She became a lot more skeptical after that." Jackson reaches out to Rose three weeks before he's scheduled to sit down with Lesley, the account manager for his preferred bidder. He invites her to lunch at his favorite Italian restaurant. It's a Friday, and the workweek is mostly behind them. They chat about Rose's two children and Jackson's prize dachshund. They discover shared passions in the Los Angeles Lakers and Broadway musicals. As they scan the dessert menu, Jackson turns to business.

Jackson: Look, Rose, I'm really interested in your thoughts about the bidders on our thin client server. I know you've got a ton of experience when it comes to local area networks, so your opinion will carry a lot of weight.

Rose: I appreciate that. . . . Have you tried the ricotta cheesecake here?

Jackson: It's fabulous—you'll love it! At this point my department is leaning toward High Performance Systems. We've worked with them before, and they've got a strong track record for quality work delivered on time and under budget. Their service is topnotch; their word is their bond. I know we'll all be able to sleep at night if they get the job. But we've got plenty of time to decide, and I didn't want to proceed without input from you and our other core stakeholders.

Rose: To be honest, I'm not so sure about High Performance Systems, Jackson. They do excellent work, no question. But when I looked over the bids, I must tell you I was impressed by Good Enuf's pricing. Just $295,000! We could save a bundle with them.

Jackson: I can't argue with you there. If it was only a question of price, they'd have the inside track.

Rose: I'm thinking we shouldn't need to go much above $300,000.

Jackson: My question on Good Enuf is whether they have the experience and staffing to guarantee that our network stays up and running. They're awfully new to the game, and you know better than I do the mortality rate for startups. Are we sure Good Enuf will be around in three years, when we'll be needing their warranty support?

Rose: That's a fair point, but we're talking about a $65,000 spread. I'm willing to take some risk for that kind of money.

Jackson: Exactly—it's all about risk and reward. I ran into our lead engineer the other day and asked him how much it would cost the company if our network went down. You know what he told me? Frankly, I was surprised—it's $35,000 a day! If we stay down two days, that wipes out the differential and then some. And when I heard that Good Enuf subcontracts out their service. . . .

Rose: (*Spooning into her cheesecake.*) Really? I didn't know that. I've had some dodgy experiences with subs in the past. It can be a real accountability problem.

Jackson: Yeah, I have to admit, that made me a little nervous, too. Look, Rose, I can see that pricing matters to you. If you don't mind my asking, how is your department doing with its budget? I know they run a tight ship around here.

Rose: Well, since you ask, we did have some unexpected personnel expenses last month. Money's going to be tight for us till the fall.

Jackson: I hear you. Look, I've got an idea. What if I could wangle some extended payment terms from High Performance? That would get you some breathing room on the budget side, and we could *all* sleep better at night.

Rose: You know what, I think I could live with that deal. Though I'd appreciate it if you could get them down to $350,000.

Jackson: I think we might even do a little better than that—you and I both know there's some padding in that bid. Just promise me one thing. If we go with High Performance and they don't meet your expectations, I want to hear about it—right away. Don't be a stranger.

Rose: (*Warmly.*) Jackson, this could be the beginning of a beautiful friendship!

How did Jackson bring Rose around to his position? Let us count the ways. He consulted her early in the game, when both of them felt less pressured to get their way. He broke the ice with nontask talk in a relaxed environment. He respectfully acknowledged her expertise. He asked thoughtful questions—both outside and inside the meeting—to get a better handle on her needs. He offered a quantified value proposition to overcome her reservations. Finally, for insurance, he gave her a full-bore forewarning. Jackson didn't shy away from his differences with Rose. Nor did he try to bulldoze over them. He used his creative conflict toolkit to arrive at a superior solution for all concerned.

Relationships feed on empathy—not empty shows, but the genuine article. When we learn what makes other people tick, we can respond to them as human beings. Once we demonstrate that we'll take care of them, come what may, it's so much easier to get them to "yes." Mutual trust is a powerful force.

When the waiter brought their check, Jackson tried to grab it. But Rose insisted on an even split. She'd already launched her transition from internal client to internal *partner*, the strategic ally that every creative negotiator needs.

Summary

- In internal negotiations, relationships are always primary. The goal is a long-term alliance. If your internal partner proves untrustworthy, you can pull back to a more skeptical posture later on.

- Your colleagues' buy-in is essential to success at the bargaining table. It's wise to build rapport with stakeholders *before* a negotiating crunch, and to get their input before handing them a fait accompli.

- Internal discovery will clarify your stakeholders' needs—and possibly reveal an important factor you'd overlooked.

- Never drift into an internal negotiation. Plan for it as you would for an external one. Determine your leverage. Set a starting anchor, a fallback, and a walkaway point. In the spirit of matching, consider how the stakeholder might reciprocate for any concessions you make.

Thinking Like a Negotiator

Readers looking for words to live and work by might consider these attributed to Aristotle: "You are what you repeatedly do. Excellence, then, is not an act but a habit."

While we've done our best to share our framework for thinking like a negotiator, there is no substitute for action. It's only through experience that people learn how to leverage their power, find common interests, and engineer a more comprehensive deal. It takes time to understand and overcome the subjective blocks that hold us back. Remaking one's mindset isn't an overnight affair.

If you're ready to give creative conflict a whirl, you might start in a lower-stakes setting—a flea market, for example, or an appliance store. Or, for the brave at heart, a homework negotiation with your children. (If you can pass that acid test, nothing in the business world will throw you.)

Psychologists refer to "the four stages of competence,"[1] a hierarchy of mastery:

- **Unconscious incompetence,** where you don't know what you don't know

- **Conscious incompetence,** where you know what you don't know

- **Conscious competence,** where you know what you're doing but need to focus to do it

- **Unconscious competence,** where a skill is so ingrained that it's now second nature

As you practice creative negotiating, and it becomes a part of your automatic system, the more unconsciously competent you will become. You'll be quicker to spot solutions that add value for both sides. As you lean into conflict and gain more positive results, you'll develop the confidence to handle high-pressure situations. You'll know instinctively what to do. You won't just be thinking like a negotiator—you will *be* a negotiator.

To speed you on your way, we'll close with a compendium of reminders:

- Carve out time to plan. The stronger your framework going in, the more freely you'll be able to improvise without losing track of your objectives.

- As part of your planning process, consider where the negotiation lies on the continuum. Then formulate your strategies and tactics accordingly.

- Activate your negotiator's mental model to aim high and proceed with confidence.

- Recognize when you're approaching a negotiating situation, even in a casual setting. Don't drift into a negotiation; be purposeful.

- Always be willing to ask for concessions. Moreover, understand *why* it's okay to ask.

- Differences are the mother's milk of added value. We can debate without making enemies.

- Try to contain the emotions that conflict tends to trigger: anger, fear, anxiety.

- Use your negotiating vision to look for larger possibilities in a deal.

- In the heat of the fray, keep your wits about you. Weigh your response before reacting.

- Think in a more flexible, nonformulaic way.

- Be patient in working the process, rather than rushing to finish and be done with it.

- Stay balanced. Steer clear of extremes.

- While partisanship is seductive, it limits a deal's upside. The best negotiators see things from the other side's perspective as well as their own.

NOTES

Preface

1. Paul Trachtman, "Matisse & Picasso," *Smithsonian Magazine*, February 2003, https://www.smithsonianmag.com/arts-culture/matisse-picasso -75440861/.
2. William Rick Fry, Ira J. Firestone, and David L. Williams, "Negotiation Process and Outcome of Stranger Dyads and Dating Couples: Do Lovers Lose?" Taylor & Francis, June 7, 2010, https://www.tandfonline.com/doi/abs/10.1207 /s15324834basp0401_1.

Chapter 1

1. The W. Edwards Deming Institute, "Quotes," 2021, https://deming.org /quotes/10083/.
2. Quoted in Chris Heivly, "Richard Branson's 1 Rule for Embracing Change," Inc.com, January 14, 2016, https://www.inc.com/chris-heivly/richard-branson-s -one-rule-for-embracing-change.html.
3. Roger Fisher and William Ury, *Getting to Yes* (New York: Penguin, 2011), 11.
4. Fisher and Ury, *Getting to Yes*, 83.
5. Fisher and Ury, *Getting to Yes,* 84.

Chapter 3

1. David Brooks, "At the Edge of Inside," *New York Times*, June 24, 2016, https://www.nytimes.com/2016/06/24/opinion/at-the-edge-of-inside.html.
2. Leslie A. Perlow and Stephanie Williams, "Is Silence Killing Your Company?" *Harvard Business Review*, May 2003, https://hbr.org/2003/05/is-silence -killing-your-company.
3. Richard Thaler, "Unless You Are Spock, Irrelevant Things Matter in Economic Behavior," *New York Times*, May 8, 2015, https://www.nytimes.com /2015/05/10/upshot/unless-you-are-spock-irrelevant-things-matter-in-economic -behavior.html.
4. Dan Ariely, *Predictably Irrational* (New York: HarperCollins, 2009), 75.
5. Daniel Kahneman, *Thinking, Fast and Slow* (New York: Farrar, Straus and Giroux, 2013).
6. Adam Grant, *Give and Take* (New York: Penguin, 2014).
7. Grant, *Give and Take*, 10.
8. Adam Grant, "Unless You Are Oprah, 'Be Yourself' Is Terrible Advice," *New York Times,* June 4, 2016, https://www.nytimes.com/2016/06/05/opinion/sunday /unless-youre-oprah-be-yourself-is-terrible-advice.html.

9. Stephen M. R. Covey, *The Speed of Trust: The One Thing That Changes Everything* (Alpharetta, GA: FranklinCovey, 2008), 125.

10. O. M. Razumnikova, "Divergent Versus Convergent Thinking," in *Encyclopedia of Creativity, Invention, Innovation and Entrepreneurship*, edited by E. G. Carayannis (New York: Springer), 362.

11. Hence the ZOPA, or zone of possible agreement.

12. Kahneman, *Thinking, Fast and Slow*, 114.

13. R. K. Cooper, *The Other 90%: How to Unlock Your Vast Untapped Potential for Leadership and Life* (New York: Currency, 2002).

14. David Brooks, "At the Edge of Inside," *New York Times*, June 24, 2016.

15. Richard Rohr, *The Eight Core Principles* (Cincinnati, OH: Franciscan Media, 2013).

16. Richard Rohr, "The Right Questions," *Third Way*, Summer 2006, 26.

Chapter 4

1. William Anton, *Business Success Through Self-Knowledge* (Lutz, FL: COEFFECTIVENESS LLC, 2013), 27.

2. "John Wanamaker," Who Made America? PBS, accessed December 17, 2020, https://www.pbs.org/wgbh/theymadeamerica/whomade/wanamaker_lo .html.

3. Daniel Goleman, *Emotional Intelligence* (New York: Bantam, 2020), 53–54; emphasis added.

4. Carol Dweck, *Mindset: The New Psychology of Success* (New York: Ballantine, 2007).

5. Richard Thaler and Cass Sunstein, *Nudge* (New York: Penguin, 2009), 33.

6. Goleman, *Emotional Intelligence*, 53.

7. William Ury, *Getting Past No* (New York: Bantam, 1993), 36–38.

Chapter 5

1. *Monty Python's Life of Brian*, directed by Terry Jones (London: HandMade Films, 1979).

2. Katie Shonk, "What Is Anchoring in Negotiation?" (Presentation at Program on Negotiation, Boston, MA, Harvard Law School, November 19, 2019).

3. *National Lampoon's Vacation,* directed by Harold Ramis (Burbank, CA: Warner Bros., 1983).

4. Arthur Miller, *The Price* (New York: Penguin, 1985), Act 1.

5. Daniel Kahneman, *Thinking, Fast and Slow* (New York: Farrar, Straus and Giroux, 2013), 123–124.

6. Robert Cialdini, *Pre-Suasion* (New York: Simon & Schuster, 2016), 5.

7. Dan Ariely, *Predictably Irrational: The Hidden Forces That Shape Our Decisions* (New York: Harper Perennial, 2010), 32.

8. William Ury, *The Power of a Positive No: Save the Deal, Save the Relationship—and Still Say No* (New York: Bantam, 2008), 61.

9. *Planes, Trains and Automobiles*, directed by John Hughes (Los Angeles: Paramount Pictures, 1987).

10. "Teaching Tales: The Way You Like It," beliefnet.com, accessed January 26, 2021, https://www.beliefnet.com/love-family/parenting/2000/10/teaching-tales -the-way-you-like-it.aspx.

Chapter 6

1. *Monty Python's Life of Brian*, directed by Terry Jones (London: HandMade Films, 1979).

2. "Tips From the Very Top: 10 Leadership Insights from Legendary GE CEO Jack Welch," *Business Insider Australia,* June 28, 2015, https://www.businessinsider.com.au/jack-welch-leadership-insights-2015-9.

3. Sometimes you don't have to say a word. Once we were in a negotiation where our team leader's undergarment started riding up on him. He rose from his seat to make an adjustment, and the other side said, "Hold on, I think we can do a little better than that."

4. Leonard J. Marcus and Barry C. Dorn, "The Walk in the Woods: A Step-by-Step Method to Guide Interest-Based Negotiation and Conflict Resolution," *Negotiation Journal*, July 12, 2012.

5. Mott the Hoople (Ballad of) Rockumentary, https://www.youtube.com/watch?v=ihZyRl3xgAE, approx. time 30:10.

6. *Shark Tank,* Season 5, Episode 21, March 21, 2014.

Chapter 7

1. As we'll see, value mapping is even more critical in creative dealmaking, where it becomes a mutual exploration of possible tradeoffs to expand the deal and add overall value.

Chapter 8

1. Daniel Kahneman, *Thinking, Fast and Slow* (New York: Farrar, Straus and Giroux, 2013), 304.

2. Adrienne W. Fawcett, "The Marketing 100: Starbucks: Scott Bedbury," *AdAge*, June 30, 1997, https://adage.com/article/news/marketing-100-starbucks-scott-bedbury/72188.

3. PRNewswire-FirstCall, "Starbucks and United Airlines Enter into Three-Year Supply and Marketing Agreement," flyertalk, August 18, 2004, https://www.flyertalk.com/forum/united-mileage-plus-pre-merger/347292-starbucks-united-airlines-enter-into-three-year-supply-marketing-agreement.html?styleid=22.

4. Angelica LaVito, "Starbucks Is Opening a Store in China Every 15 Hours," cnbc.com, December 5, 2017, https://www.cnbc.com/2017/12/05/starbucks-is-opening-a-store-in-china-every-15-hours.html.

5. "5 Cities with the Most Starbucks," TravelTrivia, September 3, 2019, https://www.traveltrivia.com/cities-with-most-starbucks-coffee/XqgZkXU1XQAGkiO8.

6. William Anton, *Business Success through Self-Knowledge* (Lutz, FL: COEFFECTIVENESS LLC, 2013), 47.

7. Stuart Diamond, *Getting More: How You Can Negotiate to Succeed in Work and Life* (New York: Currency, 2012), 34.

8. Richard Rohr, *The Eight Core Principles* (Cincinnati, OH: Franciscan Media, 2013).

9. William Ury, *The Power of a Positive No: Save the Deal, Save the Relationship—and Still Say No* (New York: Bantam, 2008), 236.

10. Paul Allen, *Idea Man* (New York: Penguin, 2011).

Chapter 9

1. Phil Rosenthal, "NBC Hopes NFL Deal Lights Way to Ratings Revival," *Chicago Tribune*, July 30, 2006, https://www.chicagotribune.com/news/ct-xpm -2006-07-30-0607300071-story.html.
2. Rosenthal, "NBC Hopes NFL Deal Lights Way."
3. Rosenthal, "NBC Hopes NFL Deal Lights Way."
4. Daniel Pink, *To Sell Is Human* (New York: Riverhead, 2012), 128.
5. Pink, *To Sell Is Human*, 68.
6. Adam Grant, *Give and Take: Why Helping Others Drives Our Success* (New York: Penguin, 2014), 151.
7. Adam Grant, *Give and Take*, 150, 152–153.
8. Eric Schmidt and Jonathan Rosenberg, *How Google Works* (London: John Murray, 2015), 184.
9. Howard Van Zandt, "How to Negotiate in Japan," *Harvard Business Review,* November 1970.

Chapter 10

1. Frank Mobus and Brad Young, "Creating Leverage," *Supply Chain Management Review*, May/June 2017.
2. Stephen M. R. Covey, *The Speed of Trust: The One Thing That Changes Everything* (New York: Free Press, 2018), xxv.
3. Robert Axelrod, *The Evolution of Cooperation* (New York: Basic, 1984), 177–178.
4. Covey, *The Speed of Trust*, xxv.
5. Daisuke Wakabayashi and Jack Nicas, "Apple, Google and a Deal That Controls the Internet," *New York Times*, October 25, 2020, https://www.nytimes.com /2020/10/25/technology/apple-google-search-antitrust.html.
6. Wakabayashi and Nicas, "Apple, Google and a Deal That Controls the Internet."
7. Carl Dahlman, "The Problem of Externality," *Journal of Law & Economics* 22, no. 1 (April 1979): 141–162.
8. Christian Annesley, "Outsourcing Works Better When Based on Trust, Survey Finds," computerweekly.com, November 24, 2005, https://www.computer weekly.com/news/2240075954/Outsourcing-works-better-when-based-on-trust -survey-finds.
9. Berkshire Hathaway, Inc., *2003 Annual Report* (Omaha, NE: Warren E. Buffett, 2004), https://www.berkshirehathaway.com/2003ar/2003ar.pdf.
10. Adam Grant, *Give and Take: Why Helping Others Drives Our Success* (New York: Penguin, 2014), 199, 213–214.
11. Daphne de Marneffe, "The Secret to a Happy Marriage Is Knowing How to Fight," *New York Times*, January 12, 2018, https://www.nytimes.com/2018/01/12 /opinion/sunday/engagement-marriage-conflict.html.

Chapter 12

1. James Surowiecki, *The Wisdom of Crowds* (New York: Anchor, 2005), 11.
2. Surowiecki, *The Wisdom of Crowds,* 31.
3. Surowiecki, *The Wisdom of Crowds*, 65.

4. Surowiecki, *The Wisdom of Crowds,* 71.

5. Surowiecki, *The Wisdom of Crowds*, 43.

6. Surowiecki, *The Wisdom of Crowds,* 187.

7. Robert Cialdini, "Harnessing the Science of Persuasion," *Harvard Business Review*, October 2001.

8. Adam Grant, *Originals: How Non-Conformists Move the World* (New York: Penguin, 2016), 185.

9. Rebecca Shambaugh, "How to Unlock Your Team's Creativity," hbr.org, January 31, 2019, https://hbr.org/2019/01/how-to-unlock-your-teams-creativity.

10. *The Free Dictionary* by Farlex, s.v. "Harry S. Truman," accessed 1/26/21, https://encyclopedia2.thefreedictionary.com/33rd+President+of+the+United +States.

11. Roger Schwarz, "What the Research Tells Us about Team Creativity and Innovation," hbr.org, December 15, 2015, https://hbr.org/2015/12/what-the -research-tells-us-about-team-creativity-and-innovation?autocomplete=true.

12. Grant, *Originals*, 198.

13. Daniel Kahneman, *Thinking, Fast and Slow* (New York: Farrar, Straus and Giroux, 2013), 264.

14. Surowiecki, *The Wisdom of Crowds*, 203.

15. Grant, *Originals*, 193.

16. Surowiecki, *The Wisdom of Crowds*, 177.

17. Leslie A. Perlow and Stephanie Williams, "Is Silence Killing Your Company?" *Harvard Business Review*, May 2003.

Chapter 13

1. Leslie A. Perlow and Stephanie Williams, "Is Silence Killing Your Company?" *Harvard Business Review*, May 2003.

2. Robert Cialdini, "Harnessing the Science of Persuasion," *Harvard Business Review OnPoint*, October 2001.

3. Perlow and Williams, "Is Silence Killing Your Company?"

Afterword

1. Beth Ferester & Company, "The Four Stages of Competence," 2018, https:// ferester.com/four-stages-of-competence/.

INDEX

ACKNOWLEDGMENTS

Creative Conflict is the product of many years of collective activity and of insights from friends, associates, and clients. For their staunch support in developing the ideas in this book, the authors would like to thank Dennis Bain, Wendy Baker, Patrick Clawson, Ron Fleisher, Michael Gillespie, Rose Greenman, Howard Hertz, Nathan Hertz, Jim Holmes, Karryn Hudson, Marc Jablon, Chet Karrass, Mel Klayman, Howard Levy, Alexandra Lubenova, Michelle Macedo, Genelle Padilla, Stephen Templeton, Karen Twersky, and Brad Young.

We're also grateful to the talented, hard-working team at Harvard Business Review Press, beginning with our editor, Jeff Kehoe. Thanks also to Lindsey Dietrich, Julie Devoll, Stephani Finks, Erika Heilman, Allison Peter, Felicia Sinusas, and Alicyn Zall; and to Erin Davis and the Westchester Publishing Services crew, for their aid in copyediting and production.

We were fortunate to enlist the services of Esther Newberg, literary agent extraordinaire. Finally, the authors would like to thank Jeff Coplon, who helped us turn our vision for this volume into a living, breathing reality.

ABOUT THE AUTHORS

One of the world's top authorities on business negotiating, **FRANK MOBUS** was the founder of Mobus Creative Negotiating. In 1982, after gaining hands-on negotiating experience as a fourth-generation contractor, Mobus joined Karrass, the industry leader in business negotiating training. Within two years, he was named senior vice president. Over the next three decades, combining academic studies with an unmatched track record in on-the-ground training and consulting, Mobus spearheaded the negotiating seminar program that became the gold standard in its field. He conducted seminars for leading corporations in every major sector in the United States and around the globe, including half of the *Fortune* 500. In 2014, he put his best and freshest ideas to work at Mobus Creative Negotiating. Mobus graduated from the University of California, Irvine, and earned his master's degree from New York University.

BILL SANDERS, CEO of Mobus Creative Negotiating, joined Frank Mobus shortly after the company launched in 2014. Sanders helped build an A-list clientele, including AT&T, BorgWarner, Skanska, and the SLAC National Accelerator Laboratory at Stanford University. Previously, as director of program development at Karrass, he created customized negotiating programs for the company's top accounts. Together with Frank Mobus, Sanders reinvented negotiating practice for the world's top companies, leading to positive and fundamental changes in how to go about making long-term agreements. Sanders received his undergraduate degree from California State University, Fullerton, and a doctorate in physical chemistry from the Pennsylvania State University. Using tools and methods first developed by his long-time associate and mentor, Bud Goode, he continues to consult with National Football League franchises on sports statistics analysis. Over the last thirty years, this work has helped NFL head coaches take their teams to ten Super Bowls.